DEBTONATOR

DEBTONATOR

How Debt Favours the Few
and Equity Can Work For All of Us

Andrew McNally

First published 2015 by
Elliott and Thompson Limited
27 John Street, London WC1N 2BX
www.eandtbooks.com

ISBN: 978-1-78396-165-8

A catalogue record for this book is available from the
British Library.

Typesetting: Marie Doherty
Printed in the UK by TJ International Ltd.

For Jessica, Michael and Sophia

Contents

Introduction

It is absurd to entrust the defence of a country to men who own nothing in it.
Diodorus Siculus, 60–30BC[1]

We are in an age of financial extremes. Since the 1970s the Western world has seen the most prolonged rise in inequality, both in income and wealth, since the 1800s. At the same time, government, household and company debt in total has become more prolific relative to income than at any time in history; it plagues our financial system and, although it might look to many like governments and central banks have the worst effects under control, indebtedness is still increasing for the world as a whole. Despite many explanations of income disparity, the causes of inequality in wealth are not widely understood. The concurrent rise in debt and wealth inequality is curious, however; this book offers one explanation of why the two might be linked.

UK prime minister Harold Macmillan famously said that 'most of our people have never had it so good'. He made that statement in the 1950s and most people have it even better today, at least economically. The wealth produced by post-war industrial recovery, together with the welfare state, improved the lot of the vast majority. In recent years, though, the economy has not been working for everyone in the way we were led to believe it would – not just by politicians but also by the economic theories that define their debates. As in the early part of the last century, those at the bottom and in the middle of society are being left behind by those at the very top. The UK economy is almost half as big again as it was in 1994 and yet, for those who are somewhere in the middle, incomes have gone up by just a fifth; they have actually flat-lined since 2002.[2] The bottom 25 per cent of American workers haven't had a real wage increase in twenty-five years.

The year 2014 was a tough one for 113 American billionaires who failed to secure a place on the Forbes 400, the prestigious list of the wealthiest people in the United States; as the stock market reached new highs, the competition simply pulled too far ahead. They should have moved to the UK; with only 107 billionaires, the slightly less prestigious *Sunday Times* Rich List left plenty of space.[3] The wealth of the top 1 per cent has been growing at a much steeper rate than anyone else's. In *The New Few*, Ferdinand Mount wonders if this is down to 'an undiagnosed malfunction or a series of malfunctions'.[4] He is right to wonder; the system is malfunctioning and it is allowing those at the top to leave the rest behind – way behind.

There's a debate raging right now about the role central banks have played in the creation of inequality.

While the central bankers themselves claim their actions prevented a second Great Depression others, both on the left and the right, focus on the impact they have had on the value of assets held mainly by the wealthy. So-called quantitative easing involved the central banks buying bonds and other assets in an attempt to free up cash in the banking system and the real economy. This is a valid debate but it says nothing of the more powerful and enduring forces that are the subject of this book. A relentless increase in the use of debt, especially amongst corporations, I argue, is a crucial link in the creation of wealth inequality; our faith in debt has left ownership of the most productive wealth, shares in companies, in the hands of the few.

Priorities change in politics; it's the nature of the beast. There was a time when ownership was the big agenda, not just of homes but of everything. The UK's early privatisation programme, for example, may have been mainly designed to offload corporations from the state and subject them to the free market, but the opportunity to create a new shareholding class was not overlooked; the 'If you see Sid ... Tell him!' campaign during the privatisation of British Gas remains an iconic moment in stock market history nearly thirty years later. Sid, however, didn't keep his shares for long and the dream of a stake-holding society never became reality.

Politicians are often playing catch-up. Keith Joseph, one of the key architects of Thatcherism, for example, broke ground in 1974 with his famous Preston speech,

'Inflation is Caused by Governments'. It was a challenge to both sides of the political spectrum after successive governments had relied on money creation to solve our economic woes and, although his speech rocked the political establishment, it addressed an issue that was becoming apparent almost ten years before. In a similar way, we need to admit that extreme inequality today, to a large degree, is caused by our financial system; to acknowledge that central banks with governments by their side, at least in their current form, are part of the problem.

In the autumn of 2011, seventy Harvard students walked out of the esteemed university's Economics 10 course. It's the course that covers the basics – the fundamentals of economic theory. 'Harvard graduates have been complicit and have aided many of the worst injustices of recent years. Today we fight that history,' said one of the dissenters at the time.[5] They see where the theory is lacking while their professors stick doggedly to the established syllabus.

We often forget that finance exists because of us, that we created it; we established the rules by which it works and which allowed it to thrive in the first place. Since the 1500s, when the Christian church found a way for Jewish money-lenders to bypass usury laws,[6] we have continuously shaped finance; learning new lessons, new flaws and new approaches. Nothing in finance occurred in nature; we can deconstruct it and reconstruct it to serve our needs.

In this book I argue that the use of equity, not debt, as a means of financing companies should be a key ingredient in the fight against the growing inequality that we are witnessing in the West. Equity, in the financial sense, is two things at the same time: it is both an investment and a rich source of finance. Equity finance, when companies sell a share in their future success, is often seen as the poor cousin of debt finance, the source of funding a company resorts to only when it really has no other choice. On its page on equity, Wikipedia describes equity investors as the 'most junior class' of investors; however, equity is the only way to invest in new real wealth creation. Technically speaking, equity holders receive a return on their investment that varies according to the performance of a firm. In practice, equity represents a share in success – in the success of a company; in the success of an economy. It is the best means by which the wealth created by the growth in the value of assets can be distributed more widely in society.

After the financial crisis of 2008, like the Harvard students, many in business and banking glimpse a different model for finance – while governments and central banks perform CPR on the old one. The foundations of the next version of global finance need to be built on equity not debt. Equity, although less commonly understood, I believe embodies the more positive and potent traits of capitalism. An economic future secured through equity will be fairer, more stable, more optimistic and more productive. Equity finance, to my mind, brings advantages for everyone that current theory does not account for; it brings benefits to companies, to owners and to society as a whole. Equity as a dominant source of finance can make us all better off.

This book begins by describing, in simple terms, what equity in the financial sense really represents as a form of wealth and as a source of finance. I then show how equity as a form of finance works in ways beyond those accounted for by established financial theory. A simple notion of the theories that have dictated how we think about equity, particularly in relation to debt, and why they might be fundamentally flawed, is essential for my argument. Debt's primacy is now hard-wired into our system and so I offer an abridged account of how this happened before moving on to the central argument of this book – that debt favours the few. I outline the processes by which our obsession with debt has secured a system that drives ownership of the most important kind of wealth into the hands of a small group at the top. I then argue that equity at large can be much better for society, an argument that is becoming ever more vital as new technology looks set to displace workers and cut wages for some time to come. Finally, I close by suggesting what, in broad terms, could be done to leave us with an equity financed, not a debt financed, society.

There are many reasons to be positive. In his

evolutionary explanation of human success *The Rational Optimist*, science writer Matt Ridley reassures us as to why: 'The availability of almost everything a person could want or need has been going rapidly upwards for 200 years and erratically upwards for 10,000 years before that.'[7] For us to sustain this progress, however, more people need to see that optimism justified; they need to have a stake in that progress.

This short book was not written simply to tell the reader to buy shares. It is not saying companies should not use debt; it is not another call for wider employee share ownership or for a confiscation and redistribution of wealth. It is simply arguing that our system needs more equity – full stop. It is a call for more assets to be financed with equity and for more people to own them. It is written with deliberate naivety. I have largely ignored the powerful vested interests that might see the world differently. Many readers may be suspicious of the intractable relationship between those who benefit most from the current system and the political class, but, assuming such a relationship exists, it presents a challenge beyond the scope of the argument given here. My hope is that it will set people thinking, vested interests or otherwise, that there might be a better way to organise our finances – one that would harness the creative dynamism of capitalism while embracing some of the humanistic ideals of fairness and shared endeavour.

These are, of course, just ideas. Putting them into practice would require the exercise of the greatest minds in economics, business, finance and government. In itself, a shift to a financial system, and actually a new version of capitalism, with equity not debt at its core, will be the greatest of shared endeavours.

1
Debt and Equity 101

Beware of geeks bearing formulas.
Warren Buffett, 2009

Finance can often seem daunting. It is frequently presented as a myriad of complex theories, impenetrable jargon and mind-bending mathematics. Many of its concepts, however, are in essence quite simple. Most people understand clearly the concept of debt, for example; it is something that nearly everyone will have practical experience of at some point in their lives. Equity, on the other hand, is slightly more complex and less run-of-the-mill.

We normally first experience the difference between debt and equity when we buy our first home. To keep it simple: suppose we buy a house for £100,000 and take out a 100 per cent mortgage; at the start, the asset's value is £100,000, the debt is £100,000 and the equity is zero. If the house's price increases by, say, 20 per cent, and so its value rises to £120,000, our debt remains at £100,000 and our equity becomes £20,000. All of the increase in the value of the house, the asset, is reflected in the value of the equity.

It isn't always this simple. We'd rarely, for example,

buy a factory or a shopping mall ourselves; a company would do these things and we would help to finance the company. The company would be either debt or equity financed and the company would own the assets – the factory, the land it sits on, the machines that fill it and so on.

To illustrate, suppose we are introduced to Smith Ventures, a company developing genetically enhanced apple trees, which is planning to use its new technology to grow a large orchard. And then suppose we offer to fund Smith Ventures' idea with debt; we give it a loan or buy a bond, which is the same thing except a bond can be more readily sold to someone else. When we do this, the asset we own is the loan we made or the bond we bought and Smith Ventures is described as debt financed. We would, on an agreed date, get our money back with interest. We, the debt financiers, get a fixed return and Smith Ventures pays a fixed price for its funding.

If we want to fund Smith Ventures with equity, we would do so by buying shares; the shares would represent a stake in the future value of the company. After buying the shares the asset we own is equity and Smith Ventures can be described as equity financed. From then on, Smith Ventures has to pay us a share of the profit, after the debt financiers have been paid; an arrangement that carries on for as long as the orchard keeps growing apples. We have bought a share in Smith Ventures' success – forever.

Smith Ventures, of course, is earning the profit from the orchard and so the value of the orchard, what accountants would call the underlying asset, is the factor that's really increasing in value. In fact, the value of the company's equity could be said to be the difference between the value of the orchard minus the value of the company's debt – just as it was with our house. As the orchard makes more money so its value goes up. The value of the debt remains the same, however, so the value of the equity in Smith Ventures rises even more. The increase in the value of the orchard, because the genetic technology works, is completely reflected in the value of the equity.

This is, by necessity, an overly simple portrayal but whatever complex structures and instruments the financial industry invents, whether in a large public corporation or a private business, this is, in essence, how we finance everything.

A house with an orchard

When people talk about assets, especially with respect to inequality, they generally bundle them all together; houses, bonds, cash, equities, pensions, mutual funds, investment trusts, gold, silver, rare stamps, fine art and jewellery are all one and the same. They are simply added up when we compare the wealth of one family relative to its neighbours.

In reality, not all assets are the same. Take the house we bought earlier for £100,000. The house's *price*, or as we would normally say, *value*, might increase but unless we spend more money on improving it, it remains the same house for the time we own it.[8]

Now take Smith Ventures. Suppose it grows its orchard and starts to yield and sell even more apples than it thought it would – its new technology turns out to be even better than at first thought. With the additional revenue it can plant more apple trees, or perhaps further develop its technology; the asset, the orchard, starts to grow in value.

Economists call the orchard and Smith's special technology 'productive assets' because they generate more wealth in ways that 'non-productive assets' cannot. 'Apple trees', though, come in all shapes and sizes: robots that build cars, research labs that discover new drugs, social networks that bring people and their ideas together. They are the things that take us forward, that drive progress. By their nature they change and, more often than not, grow as a result of things happening to or being done to them. Non-productive assets, on the other hand, may go up and down in price, they may extract a rent, but they do not create more real wealth in their own right. Bonds, houses, gold and fine art all have value but they do not change their intrinsic value in the way that Smith Ventures' apple trees can.

If you know someone who's extremely wealthy – even if only from the news – ask yourself how he or she did it. They may have made it as a popstar or footballer; they may have built up a portfolio of buy-to-let apartments. I'd hazard a guess, though, that they own a successful business, or at least a big slice of equity in one – they most likely own some 'apple trees'.

If productive assets are the only assets that create new material wealth, then how those assets are financed is crucial. I will later show how, by being debt financed, their ownership is concentrated in the hands of the few. In addition, however, the foundations of financial theory have left many corporations with the belief that debt finance doesn't impact their underlying value; that whether they survive or thrive is not determined by how they are financed. In practice, it seems their choice of finance does matter. It seems that equity finance brings value to their firms that the theory doesn't account for.

2
The Real Value of Equity Finance

Yet beautiful and bright he stood, As born to rule the storm; A creature of heroic blood, A proud though childlike form.

Felicia Hemans, Casabianca, 1826

Samuel Budgett, *The Successful Merchant* whose posthumous biography ran to forty editions, personified business values throughout the Victorian era. Having started from the small shop his father bought in 1801, his chain of wholesale grocers eventually stretched across much of England. By the time he died in 1851 he was reportedly giving £2,000 each year to good causes, a significant amount in his day. Even by today's standards a number of his business practices would be enlightened, although the thirty-minute prayer service each morning would be difficult to uphold. One such practice, however, defined his success: he would never allow his customers, or his company, to borrow. If they did, he believed, they would never stop. He wanted to show what could be achieved without debt. He left the company so financially secure that it outlasted him by a hundred years.[9]

Some of those that have fallen into the debt trap

since Budgett's day would surprise us all. Founded in 1931, Swissair flew its nation's flag like no other airline; for sixty years it was the epitome of Swiss financial prudence and was known as 'the flying bank'. There is, however, an economic theory that says stability breeds instability and Swissair was the corporate proof. In the 1990s it adopted a new approach, what it called 'the Hunter Strategy' – buying stakes in other airlines around the world with debt. By 2001 its balance sheet was loaded with close to $10 billion worth of debt, just as two planes were flown into the World Trade Center. The collapse in air travel occurred just at the wrong time for them; by October 2001, the bankers to the airline refused to refinance its debt – the airline was grounded and 39,000 passengers around the world were stranded. The BBC's business correspondent at the time summed up the gravity of the collapse well: 'Something did die in Switzerland that day: not just an airline but an image the Swiss had of themselves.' Budgett would have found the mere existence of the modern airline industry unimaginable but, since the start of commercial air travel, more than a thousand European airlines have appeared and disappeared one way or another. It has proven to be the ideal laboratory for testing his beliefs on debt and, as I will later exemplify, an ideal showcase for the power of equity finance.

A banker's first instinct these days is to advise a company, particularly if large and successful, to use debt; it's how bankers make most of their money and, on the face of it, is simple to arrange. Taken together, companies around the world have become even more indebted since the crisis: at the turn of the millennium they had $26 trillion worth of debt in aggregate; by 2007 they had $38 trillion; but by the end of 2014 their debts had risen to $56 trillion.[10] Some companies, however, ignore the bankers' advice and have avoided the seductive power of debt finance; they take a different view. For them, using mainly equity isn't 'inefficient' – as bankers often describe it – rather, it captures something different. The stability that equity finance brings allows companies to achieve things they couldn't otherwise; it makes for better decisions, permits adversity and improves the chance of long-term survival. Payback day for an equity financier is not rigid in the way that it is for debt finance; if times are tough, then an equity financier waits longer for their return. That's the deal.

When it comes to equity finance, the sense of shared endeavour can even change the behaviour of external financiers. It's no accident that in company law shareholders are also called members; when they subscribe for shares they acquire a common purpose. Small companies that use equity finance say it's good for business; advice, skills, contacts and contracts all accompany a financial backer whose financial success derives from the company's success.[11] Equity is not just another form of finance – it is a partnership.

The real value of equity finance lies in the things

banks don't always account for; things best seen in practice – in the real world. The real world, these days, is a backwater in finance. It's not where collateralised-debt obligations, credit-default swaps, algorithms, dark pools and high-frequency traders reside but where real people, running real businesses with real challenges and opportunities, ply their trade. It is among these that one discerns the full value of equity – the value that Budgett may have recognised 200 years before. Equity finance brings more than money. Management guru Peter Drucker talked of good management as 'doing things right' and leadership in business as 'doing the right thing'. Equity finance, one way or another, gives business leaders the stability to do the right thing; the right thing by their customers, employees and financial backers.

The human touch

Handelsbanken has only ever cared about one thing – its customers. For over 140 years the Swedish bank has won over each of them, one by one, branch by branch, country by country. A personal relationship with its clients, in its mind, helps it serve them better and keep a tighter handle on risk when making loans. When it enters a new town it says it would like all its customers to be able to see the church spire – if they're nearby then the bank will understand them better. Its biggest shareholders, including the bank's employees, have supported its build-it-slow strategy through thick and thin. It didn't need to raise capital or turn to its government for help during the financial crisis. What Handelsbanken's shareholders support is its human approach to doing business; it works without budgets, sales targets or advertising. None of these would help it build the customer trust to which it aspires. Sadly, when it comes to trust, the bank may never achieve its ultimate ambition: they say they would like to give the customer the keys to the bank.[12]

Finance professor Anat Admati takes a common sense approach to banking and debt and states that banks need to use much more equity finance to fund the loans they make. In its simplest form, a bank's assets are these loans and it funds them by using customer deposits, by issuing bonds, by raising equity finance or, more likely, a combination of all three. A mature industrial company, Rolls-Royce say, would typically fund 25–30 per cent of its assets with equity and yet global banking regulators currently ask that banks fund just 3 per cent of their assets with equity. Admati is convinced this approach is way too risky; if a bank's assets fell in value by just 3 per cent as a result of defaults on its loans, the bank would go bust.[13] The bankers, on the other hand, are nearly unanimous in their defence of low equity ratios. Especially since the crisis, banks are in an unusual position relative to other firms; their importance for the economy as a whole has left governments, supported by taxpayers, as backstops to their debt finance. If the banks can't pay off their debts themselves, their governments will. As a consequence, the cost of their debt finance is a lot cheaper than it would be otherwise; their debt financiers will always accept a lower return if they know their debtors are covered by the government. As bankers are paid on profit and their debt funding is cheaper than it should be,[14] why would they issue more equity to finance their business?

A reliance on debt funding and many of the business practices it supported has cost most banks, in spectacular fashion, their most valuable asset – their customers' trust. What Handelsbanken shows is that building trusting relationships with customers takes time and financial stability; the stability that only comes with equity. Once the trust is won, it brings great rewards. Despite having an equity ratio more akin to that of an industrial company, Handelsbanken has consistently been one of the most profitable banks in Europe.[15]

The financial crisis led many to question the role of banks altogether. Adair Turner, the head of the UK's main financial regulator at the time, even described much of what banks do as 'socially useless'.[16] It took a crisis driven by debt, however, for us to question their purpose in this way. We often dwell on a company's profits or on the characters that run it and the mistakes they make. We rarely reflect on the contribution they make to our lives and to our society. Once again, the airline industry offers an illustration. Love it or hate it, the low-cost airline industry has transformed Europe, and actually the world, in unimaginable ways. It's been said that 'you develop a sympathy for all human beings when you travel a lot'.[17] During the twentieth century, tens of millions of people were killed in European wars; today, over 200 million people fly between its cities daily on low-cost carriers. The successful airlines are primarily equity financed, which enables them to survive the challenges that the industry regularly faces. Their financial survival may be worth more to society than we usually give them credit for.

Customers rarely flatter low-cost airlines like they did Swissair, and yet nearly 90 million of them fly between 186 towns and cities on Europe's largest, Ryanair, every year. Historically, airlines have been lousy investments. The 'Sage of Omaha', Warren Buffett, once said, 'investors have poured money into airlines and airline manufacturers for 100 years with terrible results'. As a result, when I bought shares in Ryanair in 1999[18] on behalf of the investment firm I worked for, some colleagues raised their eyebrows; at the time, it had just 21 aircraft and 4.6 million passengers – but it also had a great idea and no debt. Today, it flies over 300 aircraft on 1,600 routes between almost 60 cities. Had it been highly indebted it's hard to imagine that Ryanair would have survived the collapse in air travel after 9/11, an oil price of $140 in 2008 and the economic meltdown of 2009.

There's no better demonstration of the value of equity finance than when financiers, the equity owners, are employees themselves. Being part of something matters. Being a member of a religion, community, club or even social network makes people behave differently and feel different – even happier. The UK Employee Ownership Index paints a striking picture – since 1995 companies with high employee ownership have out-performed those with low employee ownership by a factor of two.[19] Since Employee Stock Ownership Plans (ESOPs) were introduced in the US in 1974, many studies have revealed the same result: sales go up; productivity goes up; profits go up. In addition, the more employees join the plan, the better the effect.[20]

Ryanair's chief executive Michael O'Leary visited Southwest Airlines in the 1990s – that's where he learned the tricks of the low-cost trade.[21] After being conceived on the back of a cocktail napkin in 1971, Southwest has become one of America's biggest and most admired corporations, with $16 billion worth of sales. The adage of not investing in airlines reached cult status in the Hollywood film *Wall Street* when its anti-hero Gordon Gekko professed, 'I don't like air-lines, lousy unions'. In defiance of Gekko's maxim, Southwest has remained one of the most unionised organisations in the world and yet has persistently been the most profitable airline in America for thirty-five years; it has also consistently ranked as one of the best places to work in the US. The colourful co-founder of Southwest, Herb Kelleher, well understood the power of equity for reasons other than financial stability, especially when it was in the hands of employees; each and every one of its 46,000 workers owns stock and shares some of the profits. Southwest's value as a shared endeavour falls outside the world of financial theory; to Herb, though, it's a simple way to get the best out of people: 'If they're happy, satisfied, dedicated, and energetic, they'll take real good care of the customers. When the customers are happy, they come back.'[22]

Kelleher wasn't the first to understand the value of aligning workers' income with the success of the firm. While convalescing after a riding accident, Spedan Lewis had a eureka moment; he realised that he, his brother and his father, John Lewis, earned more than the family store's other employees put together and yet his father spent a tiny portion of his wealth.[23] In 1920, along with annual leave and shortened working days, he introduced a profit-sharing scheme for all staff. Nine years later it was turned into a partnership and in 1950 all of the family's shares were handed to the retailer's employee benefits trust. The UK high street is a dangerous place. Changing trends, low margins, high rents and high levels of company debt result in a steady stream of bankruptcies and yet, in the fifty or so years since Spedan Lewis' death, the John Lewis Partnership has thrived. His dream of keeping partners' happiness at the heart of the company's strategy, with a stake in the firm's future and the power to influence it, has secured the sense of shared passion driving the company ever since.[24] John Lewis' partnership model is not the only way to give employees a stake but its success makes a good point; broader participation in financial success by employees makes a significant positive difference to the outcome.

Alignment

The financial news is often filled with shareholders working against the interests of companies and employees while the debt financiers keep a low profile. We have to ask ourselves, however, whether this is the right way around.

Harvard professor and justice expert Michael Sandel has a clear view of when markets work and when they don't; they work best when they align the interests of all parties.[25] It's a rule of thumb that applies equally well in finance. In extremis, when a company is financed purely with equity and no debt, all the financiers' interests are aligned; all the financial backers share success along with the financial challenges. Most companies, however, shirk external equity finance because they fear the loss of control, of the ability to do as they wish with the company[26] – the thought of outside shareholders perhaps not sharing their aspirations makes them uneasy. Their belief that debt finance solves this problem, however, is an illusion. Control matters most in times of stress when debt financiers assume it anyway; they have first call on the company's underlying assets when it goes bankrupt.

Often, when it reaches this point, the company is even stripped of its future.

The alignment of interests is most often questioned and debated with respect to the private equity industry in which extremely high levels of debt are frequently used. In 2014, the demise of mobile phone retailer Phones 4U provided compelling evidence of interest misalignment. Selling mobile phones is a tough business but it can be a great one when things are going well. The mobile boom that started in the 1990s saw phone retailers around the world thrive and, by getting in early, Phones 4U had become one of the UK's largest independent retailers. Once everyone had a phone the market slowed, of course, until the smartphone revolution following Apple's launch of the iPhone in 2007. It was always tough: Phones 4U's main competitor, Carphone Warehouse, was a class act, with more stores and better brand recognition, while the concentration of network operators made pricing discussions a constant battle. In 2013, two years after buying it, private equity firm BC Partners forced Phones 4U to take on another £205 million of debt,[27] which the company then used to pay a special dividend to BC, which recouped its initial investment and made a nice profit on the trade. Things can always go wrong in business but in this case a few things happened at once. As smartphones also approached saturation point, so the networks became more aggressive and Carphone Warehouse did a deal with Phones 4U's main partner.

With massive debts to service, the company was never going to be able to compete on price and it would never be able to stand up to the networks. The market may be mature for now but who knows what new gadgets will drive us back to the shops in the future. Unfortunately, Phones 4U's employees will never find out. In 2014, just over a year after BC Partners further leveraged the company, it was bankrupt.

The unseemly death of Phones 4U sparked more outrage than the average corporate bankruptcy; it even prompted one, normally right-leaning, UK newspaper to question why the British middle-classes weren't staging a revolution.[28] In many ways the term 'private equity' is a misnomer; the skill of such investors is not primarily in the use of equity but in the use of debt. They are not the same as a normal equity investor preparing for their own or someone else's retirement – a pension fund, say. It is the debt that they use which misaligns their interests with those of other investors, financiers, managers, employees and customers. The wide availability of cheap debt in recent years has significantly enhanced private equity investors' ability to do so.

Time value

The world is speeding up – for businesses, the chance of rapid success is greater now than ever, but so is the need to adapt and change. Firms need capital that stays calm; that is patient. Patient finance makes for better decisions because it makes managers calm – it stops them losing their presence of mind. With debt, the schedule for repayment is cast in stone – and the relationship is reduced to a mathematical formula; debt providers are contractually obliged to lack patience. Equity, on the other hand, is different by nature – as an open-ended contract, it permits patience without renegotiation.

There's one industry that's been speeding up for nearly fifty years: since 1965 when electronics engineer Gordon Moore predicted that the power of microchips would double every two years, the electronics industry has grown in unimaginable ways. Personal computers, mobile phones, tablets, cars, washing machines; all have driven breath-taking demand for ever-faster chips. Despite Intel dominating the world market from the start – even today, nearly two in every three of the world's microprocessors are made by it – one of the industry's greatest success stories is that of UK chip designer ARM Holdings. Having started out in a converted barn in 1990, with £1.5 million of cash from Apple and twelve engineers, ARM always had financial prudence at heart; its first chief executive is reported to have won the firm's first boardroom table in a coin toss with a local furniture salesman. By 1993 the company was already turning a profit and in 1998 it raised nearly £40 million of new equity capital by simultaneously listing on the London Stock Exchange and NASDAQ. Its history since makes Moore's Law appear positively pedestrian: today the company has a market value of over £14 billion and its designs are the world standard for low-powered microprocessors, particularly useful in the burgeoning market for tablets and smartphones. ARM was fortunate: once it found its feet, the cash built up. It has, however, in spite of conventional thinking in finance, resisted the temptation to financially engineer itself into debt.

Although shares can change hands many times, which modern markets allow them to do almost instantly, the contracts that underlie them are permanent; the shares themselves represent ownership forever. Much of their value, therefore, is in the distant future; they discount rewards beyond the immediate. By its very nature, therefore, equity is long-term finance. In the challenging and rapidly changing world in which businesses now operate, the distraction of refinancing, of finding new debt providers, can be disruptive at the best of times. Refinancing debt at the wrong time, however, can be fatal.

The Germans have a reputation for prudence and playing a long game; the traditional image of the Swabian housewife, renowned for her hard work, thrift and ability to get the best deal, still influences German corporate culture. Daimler, Bosch and a whole swathe of German '*Mittelstand*' (small and medium-sized enterprises – SMEs) success stories were born of the inventiveness that such frugality demands.[29] The ratio of corporate debt–GDP for the industrialised world stands at around 110 per cent and yet in Germany it's 60 per cent.[30] Low debt makes sure they can keep their heads in a crisis. Swabian prudence paid off in 2009 for that most iconic of German companies, Volkswagen. In June of that year, General Motors filed for bankruptcy,[31] 101 years after it was founded. A long and difficult restructuring ensued and $51 billion of US taxpayers' money was spent on its bailout until it was returned to the stock market in 2010.[32] Many of GM's brands, including the iconic Pontiac, were discontinued and the one thing the company wasn't doing was developing new cars. That same year China became not just the fastest-growing car market in the world but also the biggest – today it's larger than the US market by a wide margin. GM's best-selling model in China, the Buick Excelle, is now over ten years old[33] but, while GM's product development stalled, Volkswagen's carried on. Today VW has by far the largest sales volume of any foreign car company in China.

One would be forgiven for thinking, while watching the business round-up on the late night news, that the stock market is important. In reality, it plays a much smaller role in our financial system than one might think. In practice, few companies seek external equity finance; for those that do, however, it's a game changer. One study of over 45,000 companies, in fifty-one countries, over a period of twenty years, showed that companies that issued bonds outgrew those relying on bank loans by 41 per cent; companies that issued equity outgrew those that relied on bank loans by 73 per cent.[34] There are two lessons here. First, that raising finance in capital markets, bond markets or stock markets, rather than relying on bank lending, has a positive impact on a company's growth. Second, that selling shares seems to have a much bigger effect than selling bonds. It is difficult, of course, to know for sure whether companies that raise capital do so because they are growing or whether the fundraising itself leads to more growth. It's a fair assumption, though, that access to capital in markets allows companies to real-ise more of their potential. It is also likely that the much higher growth seen by those companies issuing equity is, to a degree, the result of the effects discussed here: the confidence that financial stability confers on managers, the support that companies receive from external shareholders, the publicity that companies receive when listed on a stock exchange and the buy-in from employees that results when they own shares.

The idealistic version of equity depicted here is at odds with the one usually portrayed. Accounts of myopic and disengaged shareholders, tolerant of greedy management who trample over the interests of workers, customers and the environment, fill the news daily – the 'shareholder' is under attack. It seems to me we might be hanging the wrong guy. It is interesting to see growing disillusion with the role of shareholders, stock markets and equity ownership at a time when the use of corporate debt has been in ascendance. One has to wonder whether, in some way, it's the proliferation of debt that has detracted from the full value of equity finance. Is it the debt that has allowed certain equity holders, including senior management, to take more than their fair share or reap rewards before they were due?

In a world of increasing transparency, through open media and social networks, doing the right thing, as Drucker describes, is becoming a prerequisite for business success. Financing a company mainly with equity does not guarantee that management does the right thing, nor indeed success. It does, however, give the company and its management the stability to lead with patient capital, possibly with its employees alongside.

3
Nobel Finance

The ideas of economists and political philosophers,
both when they are right and when they are wrong,
are more powerful than is commonly understood.
Indeed, the world is ruled by little else.
John Maynard Keynes, 1936

In 2009, the *Harvard Business Review* published a blog, 'When is debt good?'[35] by two financial experts explaining why it was bad for Google not to have debt. To help their case, they described a meeting with the employees of a small business that was being bought by a large public one. The owner of the small business was concerned. 'Why do we have debt in this new company? I hate debt,' he protested. The experts went on to explain to the worried employees why companies should have debt. First, they argued, debt finance is cheaper because companies get tax relief on the interest costs and, second, equity is more expensive than debt because the equity investors must be compensated for accepting a higher level of risk. For the sake of their argument, they suggested that equity investors might want a 10 per cent return, whereas debt can usually be found at much lower rates. In the experts' minds, this made debt a 'bargain' – Google, and the small company they were talking to, should be financed with debt. As far as bankers and many of their corporate customers are concerned, using debt in good measure is a win–win deal – modern financial theory has made them think this way.

It has become apparent since the crisis of 2008 that finance has reached an impasse. The theories that have crafted the way we think about assets and the way we finance our 'apple trees' are not working in quite the way their creators hoped.[36] I will show later, for example, how someone investing £10,000 in equity at the age of thirty might, according to modern financial theory, receive £32,000 on retirement at sixty or they might receive £228,000 – disciples of the theories can't quite agree which.

The building blocks of modern financial theory rely on a whole number of assumptions, a few of which most people would deem to be not merely unrealistic but also bizarre. They assume, for example, that everyone can borrow unlimited amounts of money and that there are no transaction costs or taxes. They assume that, if an investment makes too much money versus other assets, it is nonetheless a risky investment, or at least according to the measures of the risk they use. They assume that we all have the same information at the same time – no one knows more than the next guy.

One assumption stands out above all others as problematic. Modern financial theory that forms the cornerstone of our system assumes a view of human nature that is simply unrealistic; it has us down as rational, selfish optimisers who can receive and dissect new information at lightning speed and use it in our own best interests. Since it was made in the early 1960s, this assumption gained an almost religious following – what rational human being would deny being rational? – but it is far from reality. Although we might be rational in a much broader sense, in a purely economic sense we are far from it. It seems, for example, that we don't value gains and losses in the same way. Suppose you have two options: option one, a 50 per cent chance of gaining £1,000 and a 50 per cent chance of gaining nothing; option two, a chance to take £500 with certainty. If you're risk averse, you choose option two; if you're not, you take your chance and choose option one. Now suppose you already have £2,000 and have two different options: option one, you have a 50 per cent chance of losing £1,000 and a 50 per cent chance of losing nothing; option two, you lose £500 with certainty. When weighted according to probability, both options are worth £1,500; however, the vast majority of people would take the second option. Unlike in the first scenario, nearly everyone plays it safe. If we were purely rational the results, when tested on real people, of both scenarios would be equal; it seems, however, that we view potential losses in a very different way to potential gains.[37] Our human nature makes us behave in a different way to the 'rational optimiser' assumed by modern financial theory. It can make us take some strange decisions; one might, for example, naturally walk for fifteen minutes to save £20 on a new £100 mobile phone but be much less likely to walk for fifteen minutes to save £20 on a £15,000 car. Rationally, £20 is £20 and fifteen minutes is fifteen minutes – but that's not how we humans think.

Keynes himself well understood the importance of the 'animal spirits' that drive our economic behaviour and, in the modern age, many understand that we have some uniquely human traits that are far from economically rational. We use rules of thumb rather than pure logic; we over-value our experiences when working out how to react to new challenges; we form stereotypes that allow us to make snap judgements; we hold on to what we have, even when it holds us back; we look for evidence to support what we think we know; we prefer fairness to selfishness; we are impatient; we are instinctive.

The foundations of modern financial theory and the assumptions they rely on created the perfect environment for an over-reliance on debt and a denial of equity ownership for the many. In corporate finance, they told us that the structure of a company's funding didn't matter; whether it used debt or equity, the value of the firm remained the same. This defined the way in which investment bankers advised, the way companies took their advice and the way investors rebuked those that didn't.

Investors and pension funds were led to believe that the future wasn't uncertain, with infinite possibilities, but was risky in a predictable way, as on a roulette table or with the shake of a dice. The risk of holding an asset was easy to measure; one simply looked at the volatility of its returns, which was assumed to be the same in the future as it was in the past. This idea was so neat it set the tone for a generation of investors. Fund managers stopped investing and began a search for what they called 'alpha', returns in excess of what was expected given an asset's volatility. Pension funds talked of 'efficient portfolios' rather than the returns to their pensioners. I will show later how this belief led to pension funds in both the UK and the US being forced by advisers and regulators to sell their clients' equity and own bonds with a much lower return.

The medieval philosopher William of Occam devised a quick method for working out which of two theories is most likely to be correct: it's the one that relies on the fewest assumptions. In common language – don't discount the obvious. The creators of modern finance who most strongly influenced our attitude to debt and equity forgot this simple trick. Their perfect world, populated by economically rational calculators working in their own self-interest, did not exist. We are, after all, human.

4
The Rise and Rise of Debt

Genius always gives its best at first; prudence, at last.
Lucius Seneca, Advisor to Emperor Nero, 4BC–AD65

It would be tempting to believe that the debts dating from before the 2008 financial crisis have gone away – they haven't. Just before the crisis, household, firm and government debt for the world in its entirety amounted to 174 per cent of global GDP; by 2014, it was 212 per cent.[38] In absolute terms, that's around $165,528,960,000,000; if we put the dollar bills end-to-end we'd get to Mars and back more than fifty times. A notion of where that journey started will help us understand how it might have gone so far.

Debt has had plenty of time to reach such primacy. Anthropologist David Graeber believes it's at least 5,000 years old and preceded money by several thousand years.[39] Although there is evidence of coinage appearing 600 years before Christ, there are debt records from the Sumerian economy of Mesopotamia, modern-day Iraq, from 3,000 years before that. Debt was more or less always on the rise, particularly following the industrial revolution. For the biggest economies, on average, it rose from 16 per cent of national output in the late 1800s to around 70 per cent in 1970.[40] This was to be expected; as more people connected as a result of urbanisation and improving communications, the more opportunities there were for more people to borrow, lend, trust, defer and invest – it's what the experts have called financial deepening.

Rapid growth in debt, particularly household debt, nearly always precedes a crisis. For example, in the nine years before the Great Depression, the invention of hire purchase agreements allowed US families to buy cars and washing machines on credit, which they did in style. In the run-up to the 2008 financial crisis, mortgages for the less well off were the innovation that propelled household debt to an astonishing new level.[41] Putting these more apparent growth spurts aside, however, there's been a more insidious advance: our current version of capitalism seems to rely on a relentless rise in debt, as evidenced by the desire of governments to keep it expanding – and available.

Debt set free

If the debt-to-GDP ratio seemed high in 1970, it's over three times that level today, at more than 200 per cent of global output; in some countries, such as the UK, it's closer to five times.[42] Debt found a whole new lease of life in August 1971; financial deepening turned into something different.

As soon as banks realised a few centuries ago

that they could lend more than they had in deposits, depending on the confidence of depositors, credit was bound to grow. Of course, when their depositors demanded more back than the banks had in reserve, then the banks would fail and so, to stabilise the system, central banks took on the role of lender of last resort. The Bank of England assumed this role in a panic in 1866 following the failure of the so-called 'bankers' bank' Overend, Gurney and Company; the US Federal Reserve was created following a panic in 1907, aptly named the 'Knickerbocker Crisis' after the New York Trust Company whose demise proved to be the last straw for an already nervous market. When an individual bank got into trouble, when its reserves ran out, the lenders of last resort could step in and maintain everyone's confidence.

Confidence, however, can soon lead to overconfidence and with the 'old lady'[43] behind it a bank could test the limits of its reserves to a much greater degree. Moreover, the confidence inspired by the central banks, on the face of it, appeared limitless; if they became overwhelmed, they could always create more money.

Monetary history has been a long battle between abstention and temptation. To pay for the mounting costs of sustaining their empire, the Romans notoriously clipped the edges from their Denarius and used the excess silver to mint new coins; the German Weimar Republic printed so many Deutschmarks that the exchange rate stood at DM4,200,000,000,000 to one US dollar by the time it finally collapsed.[44] Prudence, every now and then, gives way to improvidence.

In modern times, for a while at least, prudence was in control. A deep sense of insecurity at the end of the Second World War helped knock heads together at the Bretton Woods hotel in New Hampshire and out came the most ambitious plan for globally stable money we have ever seen. Keynes himself was one of the main architects along with US Treasury official Harry White; in total forty-four Allied nations had a hand in its construct, a key part of which would be the creation of the International Monetary Fund (IMF) and the World Bank.[45] An agreement of such magnitude, covering widely differing national situations and interests, would always require much compromise but by-and-large the American plan was the one enacted; it was, after all, the largest creditor to war-torn Europe. The Bretton Woods agreement anchored the world's major currencies, through the dollar, to gold at $35 an ounce. Not only was the dollar fixed to an asset of undoubted credibility, as gold had been the basis of the international monetary system for generations, but other major currencies were fixed to the dollar too; any change in a currency's dollar exchange rate was made subject to international approval via the IMF. In theory, it meant that countries could not allow their currencies to devalue in an attempt to become more competitive at the expense of others, or print money to pay off excessive borrowing – doing either would breach the agreement.[46]

For more than two decades it worked: stable money and post-war recovery prevailed, more or less, and faith in the dollar as the global reserve currency held strong. As war-torn industrial Europe found its feet, however, America started buying more European wares than it was selling back, just as the costs of the Vietnam War were starting to mount. As the US printed more dollars to finance its mounting debts Europeans started to worry about the value of their growing dollar reserves and began converting them into gold. President Nixon sensed the start of a run. If you're going to panic, make sure you're the first. Thus on 15 August 1971, he announced the 'closure of the gold window'; no longer could a country, or anyone else for that matter, convert its dollars to gold.

The Bretton Woods agreement was complex and, many would argue, unsustainable on the basis that too much onus was placed on the shoulders of weaker nations and not enough on the US. There was, however, a limit to how much credit individual countries could create – the link to gold dictated by the system and policed by the IMF restricted the growth of debt. Once it had broken down, governments and their central banks, unencumbered by the link to gold, could allow an expansion of credit – debt – without worrying about their obligations to defend their currency and the rate at which it was pegged to the dollar. Debt was free once more.

The perfect ally

The proliferation of debt in the Western world since the breakdown of Bretton Woods has, more often than not, been supported by central banks. Understanding central banks, however, is not an easy task. They're riddled with contradictions and interpretation of their actions is a constant source of debate. Here, I offer just one, and a very brief one at that.

In relation to borrowing, many governments lost their prudent heads post-Bretton Woods. The US, for example, had accumulated massive budget deficits[47] by the mid-1970s, which, along with inflation, was a problem mirrored in the UK. The decade of economic malaise that followed and the subsequent political bloodletting that swept the likes of Ronald Reagan and Margaret Thatcher to power eventually resulted in the monetarist revolution – a new understanding of the role of money and how it affects our economy. There was a new target for central bankers – bringing down inflation. Every salesperson will tell you that targets only ever get harder to reach; however, on this occasion, central banks got lucky. Capitalism has a deflationary side; through competition we become more efficient. As well as inventing new products, we become adept at making old ones cheaper; consider, for example, the price of the average television relative to average income over the last thirty years. When Deng Xiaoping's China decided to compete, a process that formally started in 1978[48] but which really took off in the 1980s, the world would gain a new deflationary force stronger than any in history. To meet their new inflationary targets, central bankers in the West had a tailwind stronger than they would ever have imagined – the deflationary impact of Xiaoping's China made sure they couldn't fail.

From a peak of nearly 15 per cent in 1980, US inflation steadily declined and so central bankers could turn their attention to a more worthy cause – they could focus on helping governments maintain full employment by keeping interest rates low and consumer demand high. Such demand management was one of the strategies, along with his preferred approach of increased government spending, Keynes recommended if the economy was stuck in a rut – it was his solution for the Great Depression. There are now many interpretations of Keynes and his contribution, but his ideas on demand management were the most enduring. Before his work it was assumed that the economy overall would always be in equilibrium, that great depressions couldn't really happen. From Keynes on, it was accepted that governments could and should try to manage the overall level of demand – the debate instead focused on when and how.

Alan Greenspan, Chairman of the Federal Reserve from 1987 to 2006 and known affectionately as the

'Maestro', took the view that stimulating demand when it starts to weaken, rather than waiting until the economy is in recession, was the best approach. If inflation is under control, why not cut interest rates and keep demand and output powering ahead? For a while the Maestro appeared to be right; from the time of his arrival until the financial crisis of 2008, the Western world experienced one of the most prolonged periods of high growth and low inflation in over a century – it became known as the Great Moderation.

There was one notable side effect, however. The collapse in technology shares following the dotcom boom of 2000 was brushed aside and asset prices thundered upwards, house prices flew and bond markets soared. When bond prices go up, interest rates come down[49] and so corporations, households and governments could borrow money at virtually no cost – which they did like never before.

One may wonder why the central bankers, in charge of stability, didn't worry about rocketing asset prices – but why would they? Modern financial theory told them that markets were efficient and so there was no need to worry; assets, surely, were always at the right price? The inconsistencies that permeate our central banks are now unfathomable. When things are going well, markets are efficient; when they're not going well, markets must be inefficient. When bonds are high, they're at the right price; when they weaken, they're at the wrong price.

Since the crisis, to keep prices high and the banks liquid, central banks have been buying bonds like crazy. Since 2009, the Federal Reserve has grown its balance sheet, where it holds the bonds, from $1 trillion to $4 trillion; the more modest Bank of England, from £100 billion to close to £400 billion.

With buyers like these in town, debt has the perfect ally. Central bank support for household, government and corporate borrowing is now stronger than it was before the last financial crisis.

The liquidity fetish

The financial industry has changed beyond recognition in the last thirty years; financial instruments and the markets they are traded on have become ever more sophisticated. There is a dark side, however, which, I would argue, has heavily influenced our ability to borrow. An obsession with liquidity – the ability to readily sell assets – is at the heart of the financial system and its current bias towards the use of debt.

People in the West have been developing commitment issues for some time. Around a fifth of British couples who married in the year in which the Bretton Woods system collapsed were divorced by their fifteenth wedding anniversary; of those who married in 1995, a third were divorced by the time of the financial crisis.[50] Legendary investor Peter Lynch once observed that 'ease of divorce is not a sound basis for commitment' – in this instance, though, he was referring to finance. Investors, pension funds and banks have become obsessed with the ability to sell assets before they even buy them – Keynes called it the 'liquidity fetish'. He went so far as to describe the obsession as 'anti-social'[51]; because investment institutions focus on liquidity they forget that there is no such thing as liquidity of investment for the community as a whole – not everyone can sell at the same time. If debt as an asset could always be sold to someone else, then the fear of default – of the borrower not paying back – was no longer the concern of either investors or banks. If things turned bad, it was someone else's problem. All the financial industry had to do was convince bankers and bondholders that debt could always be sold; that credit risk – risk of a loan being irrecoverable – had become merely liquidity risk: less threatening, less final.

The fetish gave birth to a whole industry supplying liquidity. Banks became traders not lenders, exchanges competed on volume and speed, and new structures were invented to separate the debtors from the ultimate lenders. Slicing, insuring and renaming credit risk became the new game in town. Collateralised debt obligations, credit default swaps, asset-backed securities – all were designed to reassure us. So long as there was liquidity, debt was safe – we could simply sell it on.

The wheel of fortune

Banks have been equally keen to use the central banks' approach to their own advantage.

If a company wants to raise equity finance, it speaks to its friendly investment bank. If the company is too small to appeal to an investment bank, it has to find a business angel or venture capitalist. But with equity, of course, comes stability – and the need for regular debt refinancing is gone: the last thing a banker needs. If a bank can borrow at, say, 1 per cent interest and lend to a company at 4 per cent, or even more if the company is weak, then better to keep that company in debt than raise all the equity it needs and bid it farewell.

Take a cursory look at income for the world's biggest investment banks. Between 1998 and 2009, they saw income grow by 11 per cent on average, well above the rest of the economy. Revenue related to debt, currencies and commodities rose five-fold, largely driven by trading debt and its derivatives. Their revenue from equities, by 2011, was less than a fifth of their overall business, on average;[52] with the exception of advisory fees, most of the rest was debt finance and debt-related trading.

Companies rarely use equity markets as a source of finance. They use bond markets more, but use neither equity markets nor bond markets as much as they do bank lending. Between 2001 and 2005, equity issuance across fifty-one countries was less than 1 per cent of GDP; even after the financial crisis when credit was meant to have been scarce, it amounted to only 1.3 per cent. Corporate bond issuance, on the other hand, was around three times that. The UK equity market has barely been a source of new finance for over a decade. In fact, more money has been taken out of companies through dividends, share buy-backs and acquisitions than has been put in through initial public offerings (IPOs) or other fund-raising procedures.[53] The number of companies listed on the main market of the London stock exchange, for example, has been steadily declining for many years. In 1999, there were close to 2,000 listed companies; now there are closer to 1,000.

The debt bias in finance, the incentives to recommend and use debt as a primary source of corporate funds, has created a wheel of fortune for the financial industry but squeezed equity out. New incentive structures and a new approach on the part of governments, regulators, advisers and corporations themselves are the only way to bring it back. The situation will take time to reverse. The belief that debt is good is now so ingrained in the fabric of many corporations that even a change in structural bias favouring equity would take time to influence behaviour.

Debt and taxes

Leaving aside credit creation, supported by central banks, there is no greater structural bias in favour of debt finance than corporate taxation; for much of the world, there is enormous support for the use of debt in corporations. Interest expenses on debt finance have been tax deductible for US corporations since 1918, when this allowance was introduced as a temporary measure to compensate company owners for an excess-profit tax.[54] When the excess-profit tax was repealed in 1921, the tax deductibility of interest mysteriously remained, without explanation. The vast majority of countries around the world now operate the same system – the incentive for companies to use debt is overwhelming. Despite tax systems already being loaded in its favour, authorities further cleared the path for debt finance. In the UK, for example, advance corporation tax – a complex system that levelled the playing field for equity finance by allowing pension funds to claim tax back on dividend income, so making equity ownership more attractive – was abolished by a Labour chancellor in 1997, a process that had been started by a Conservative chancellor in 1993 as an inconspicuous way to raise tax revenue.[55]

In the US, the BUILD (Businesses United for Interest and Loan Deductibility) Coalition is spoiling for a fight. As a few Democrat and Republican law-makers call for limits on the level of interest expenses US companies can deduct from their tax bills, BUILD senses danger. 'Any limitation to interest deductibility will only serve to raise costs on growing businesses and slow job growth,' said one of its members.[56] In practice, the tax deductibility of interest doesn't cut costs – it just incentivises the use of debt. The original justification for the tax deductibility of interest costs, known as the debt shield, is that interest is a cost of doing business whereas equity returns reflect business income. This is nonsensical from an economic perspective; debt and equity are both sources of capital for a corporation and both are paid out of the returns to that capital. There is no reason to tax them differently.

Does debt matter?

The rise and rise of debt, along with the beliefs and structural biases that have supported it, are clear to see. It is by no means assumed by all economists, however, that the debt matters at all. Many would argue that if we add up family, government and firm debt we may end up with a very large number but, unless Martians really exist and are happy to be bankers to planet Earth, the debt just nets off to zero – it is just money we owe to ourselves.[57] To these minds, one man's debt is always just another man's asset – therefore, debt is not a problem. Others would argue that because banks can create deposits and debts out of thin air,[58] the overall level of debt can go up and down in huge cycles and thus has a serious impact on the economy and asset prices, especially when it goes down (this situation is called 'debt-deflation' and is one explanation for the Great Depression).[59] Yet other economists argue that it's the distribution of the debt that matters; the trans-fer of spending power from savers to borrowers, from rich to poor, is how debt affects the way the economy works. When the poor get into trouble and the rich call in their loans, the economic consequences are very real.

Either way, to argue that debt doesn't matter is at odds with the smoking guns we see left, right and centre – not least the financial crisis. When we look at the last forty years, rather than just the period of the Great Moderation, expansion in credit has been accompanied by bouts of sluggish growth, volatile markets and extreme inequality. Even growth during the Great Moderation now appears to have been largely driven by debt and, today, asset prices are driven more by central banks than fundamental appraisal.

Debt can provide a great tailwind for economic growth and prosperity but only up to a point. Financial deepening makes sense when more families with a stable income can buy a house or a company waiting on a late payment needs some short-term financing. Beyond these more 'natural' uses of debt, however, the tailwind turns into a headwind; beyond a certain point, around 80–100 per cent of GDP,[60] debt becomes a problem.

Monetary issues are rarely recognised even by experts let alone the wider population – even when their influence is clear for all to see. One of the most accomplished accounts of hyper-inflation in the Weimar Republic talks of people blaming inflation on 'the greed of tourists, or the peasants, or the wage demands of labour, or the selfishness of the industrialists and profiteers, or the sharpness of the Jews, or the speculators making fortunes in the money markets'[61] – everyone was blamed bar the printing press. Today, we see extreme inequality blamed on globalisation, immigration, greedy bankers, corporate raiders, political corruption and biased tax systems. In the next chapter I outline how extreme inequality in wealth can largely be seen as a debt phenomenon; how our reliance on credit and the strong debt bias of our system has pushed ownership of the most important form of wealth into the hands of the few.

5
How Debt Favours the Few

The extent of and continuing increase in inequality in the United States greatly concern me.
Janet L. Yellen, Chair of the US Federal Reserve, 2014

If it's your sixtieth birthday today, you can expect to live to the age of eighty-four; that's twenty-four years of economic and social change ahead of you. A sixty year old in 1990 would, on average, have lived to see the birth of the Internet, the mobile phone, social networks, cheap air travel, electric cars, Amazon, biofuel, iPods, iPads, wind farms and unimaginable improvements in healthcare. And yet, for someone close to retiring at sixty years of age, switching into bonds with a guaranteed income is, according to perceived wisdom, the best advice.

George Ross Goobey was thirty-six years old before he was appointed pension fund manager at Imperial Tobacco, an age when many in the financial industry are seen as veterans. This was a different time, though, when most of his senior colleagues were still traumatised by two world wars and the slump of the early 1930s. In a speech to a group of pension fund trustees in 1958, he made a simple observation: shares in companies represent assets that grow and so they stood a better chance of meeting the financial needs of his pensioners. Not just that, he also realised that the dividend yield on the shares was higher than the yield on the gilt-edged bonds his colleagues all 'knew' were safe. It was a hard sell, but he clearly had all the skills you need to succeed in modern finance. Imperial Tobacco's retirees had a better old age than most, not least Ross Goobey, who retired with a handsome pension and a limitless supply of his favourite cigar.

The back-end of 2012 was a historic moment for UK pensioners. For the first time in more than half a century their retirement funds, on average, held more bonds than equities. It was an absurd set of circumstances that brought them there. The UK regulators had been arguing for some time that bonds were less risky than equities and so pension funds should hold more of them. Pension fund managers are always under pressure to make sure they can meet their financial commitments when their pensioners retire – it's the part of their job they don't want to screw up – and so they took the regulators' advice willingly; better safe than sorry. The problem was, as soon as the pension funds bought the bonds, the Bank of England was in the market to buy more itself as part of its strategy to keep the economy's credit system working[62] – driving up the price and forcing down the yield because bond prices and yields are always inversely related. Of course, as the yield fell it made the fund managers' jobs even harder – how would they meet their liabilities with the yield on bonds so low and the risk of holding equities so high? In their minds, they had no choice – they played safe and bought more bonds.

Ross Goobey's speech and the current state of pension funds are like bookends to the tale of modern finance. Modern financial theorists, however, have been puzzled for some time, even though it took them a few years to admit it.[63] If you look at all equities over a very long time period, the last century say, and examine the volatility of their returns relative to risk-free assets, like US government bonds, then 'rational' investors should have needed an additional return of around 1 per cent per year to compensate them for the additional risk. Yet, for some reason, equities have returned a lot more than that. In fact, US equities returned 7.9 per cent on average between 1889 and 2000, while US government bonds returned just 1 per cent.[64] If you'd invested £100 in UK equities in 1900 it would have been worth £28,368, in real terms, by the end of 2013; gilts – UK government bonds – would have returned just £393.[65]

Once again, it comes down to an understanding of what financial assets really represent; when you buy a bond or an equity, what ultimately are you really buying? In Debt and Equity 101, I showed how the growth of productive assets, the 'apple trees', is always reflected in equity values in a way that it is not for debt financiers. One hundred years of evidence shows that equity returns more to the owner than the owner actually needs to reward him for the risk he has borne. The evidence makes a point fundamental to the argument of this book: equity is the most effective recycler of newly created wealth; in fact, it is the only recycler of newly created wealth. Fine art may go up in price, ownership of gold might be a way to protect wealth when the world looks unstable, bonds might guarantee a return – but business equity is the only way to buy a stake in new wealth creation, the sort of wealth creation that goes hand-in-hand with human progress itself.

Most people have more immediate needs than equity ownership. Indeed, our view of ownership is such that it is, at best, an afterthought – something we seek once all other needs and wants are met. Equity as the most important recycler of wealth, of a means to a better material end, is largely neglected; instead, it is most often treated as something of a luxury. Our financial system largely facilitates this situation. For an average family there are usually ways to debt finance a new car or washing machine, and of course a house, but few ways to debt finance ownership of the assets that actually create new wealth.

Many point to pensions as the main way for people to own equity but pensions are more unequally spread than overall wealth – the top 1 per cent own nearly a quarter of all private pension wealth in the UK and yet a fifth of people close to retirement, 55–64 years old, have no private retirement pot at all.[66] Moreover, the average UK pension fund has seen its equity holdings fall from 80 per cent of total assets to less than 40 per cent today; the situation in the US is similar.[67] Pensions, it seems, are not secured by as many 'apple trees' as you might think. Unfortunately, most people will most acutely experience the result of this insecurity some way through their retirement.

Financial deepening has only gone so far. All but a tiny minority of people in the UK, for example, have a bank account and yet financial participation in a more meaningful way is surprisingly limited. A quarter of households have negative financial wealth – debt; savings and investments for those exactly in the middle amount to less than £6,000. UK families are bombarded with savings products that supposedly secure their financial future. Individual savings accounts (ISAs), for example, offer good tax incentives but in practice the actual amount accumulated in these schemes, on average, is less than £10,000; moreover, only a part of that is invested in equities. Even when people own shares directly, which around 11 per cent of households do, the average value is just £4,000.[68]

And, as it turns out, the greatest shareholding democracy on earth isn't a shareholding democracy. By 2007, more than half of all US business equity, private and public, was owned by the top 1 per cent[69] of owners; the top 10 per cent owned nearly 90 per cent of it. The difference between the top and bottom is staggering. On average, those in the top 10 per cent of business equity owners own more than 100 times what the bottom 10 per cent own.[70] Inequality in ownership of business equity is much greater than inequality in terms of overall wealth; the most important wealth of all really is owned by the few. And the situation is getting worse; a family in the middle of the top 10 per cent has seen its holdings in listed equities rise from less than $300,000 in 1989 to around $1,000,000 today. For the 20 per cent in the middle of society in terms of stock ownership, stock holdings, either direct or through funds, have risen from $32,000 to $64,000.[71] Those in the middle have benefitted from the market's rise but they haven't benefitted in the same way. It appears that owning a few productive assets might make it easier to keep acquiring more.

Most critics of capitalism will think concentrated ownership is natural – it's what happens just before the majority revolt – and Marx himself thought it was the ownership of the means of production that separated one class from another. This might be right from a purely economic point of view but capitalism isn't a purely economic phenomenon; taking democracy and capitalism together, ownership in other respects has broadened. Land reform in many parts of the world created new landowners in the nineteenth century and the democratisation of home ownership defined the twentieth century, particularly in the UK and the US. And yet, despite attempts through privatisation of state-owned companies in many parts of the world, ownership of equity hasn't spread in the same way; in fact, if anything it's gone backwards in recent years. The 'apple trees' have stayed in the hands of the few.

Denial in the new religion

This is no conspiracy theory. I foster no image of a few men in smoke-filled rooms dreaming up ways to steal our economic future. There's a paradox at work, though, that's difficult to get your head around. Modern financial theory told us that companies' debt finance didn't detract value from their firms, especially given the tax benefits; at the same time it told bankers and central bankers that debt is safe. As the total debt of governments, companies and households grew ever larger, the value of equity in general became more volatile, for the same reason that individual companies become unstable when they have too much debt. Of course, as adherents of modern financial theory, investors, particularly pension funds, believed that they therefore needed a higher return to justify holding equity – the logic that higher volatility in the past meant risk in the future guided their strategy. Rather like Ross Goobey's senior colleagues, we were back to believing that low-yielding government bonds were a better investment because they were safe.

Modern financial theory had set up the perfect financial religion – a Holy Trinity of rational investors, perfect markets and obliging central banks that would only ever lead to one outcome – more debt. Moreover, the asset that's most effective at spreading wealth, equity, was squeezed out of the system and up in to the hands of the few.

Everyone bought into the new religion. Fund managers, advisers, actuaries, regulators, corporations – everyone accepted the creed without question. Take regulators. After UK pension funds had been backed into the corner of owning low-yielding bonds, the regulator stated, 'We think that people who are making a long-term investment decision deserve to have a pretty good indication of what they are likely to get back', and instructed them to adjust their guidance accordingly.[72] On the face of it, the regulator was working in the best interests of pension holders, making sure they were properly informed. However, much lower ownership of equity was accepted without question. Regulators have become obsessed with protection; pensioners need protecting, consumers need protecting and savers need protecting. On one level they are right – protection from poor or fraudulent business practices is essential – but protection has turned to denial of equity ownership; not just in the regulatory approach to pension funds but in the setting of society's approach to risk. We have to ask ourselves if we've sleepwalked into a regulatory environment in which we discourage too many not to claim a stake in the rewards of economic progress itself. As what they call 'risk assets', a scarier way to describe equity, are deemed unsuitable for everyone apart from those who can really tolerate the 'risk', they are bought only by those with the wealth and confidence to invest in spite of the risk. Financial advisers understandably toed the line of regulators and increasingly recommended 'safer' assets to clients – for the majority, equity ownership became something they were advised to pursue as merely a supplement to other financial assets.

Although the new financial religion gave credence to the rise of debt and the denial of equity, the evidence it relies on is more spurious than you might think. Modern financial theorists have been trying to agree, for example, how much more equities should return than debt; as is common with economists, they can't. Of 150 textbooks published between 1978 and 2008, the premium ranged from 3 to 10 per cent; fifty-one of the books used different numbers on different pages[73] – they were even disagreeing with themselves in their own books. You wouldn't think the difference between three and ten could do too much damage but over time it can make all the difference. Suppose you invested £10,000 and left it for thirty years. In bonds yielding 1 per cent, you'd end up with £13,478. In equities with a 3 per cent premium, you'd end up with £32,433. With a 10 per cent premium, however, you'd end up with £228,922. As the theorists debate between themselves, the implications for everyone else can be life changing.

Tax shielded

The way pension funds work, the way savers are advised and the way regulators regulate curtails the demand for equity. Corporate tax curtails the supply of equity.

The tax shield for interest expenses on debt subsidises the returns to equity for the few who have it – and it stops business owners having to use external equity finance that would more broadly distribute the financial rewards of their success. One economist at the IMF thinks the evidence is clear: it creates 'significant inequities, complexities and economic distortions'.[74]

Business, of course, is not charity and entrepreneurial endeavour should be fairly rewarded. We should question, though, whether the tax deductibility of interest costs is fair. Does it compel those who own the assets to make sure they remain the only owners, even if doing so is not in everyone's interest, including their own?

The tax shield for corporations is one of many perverse tax incentives that pervade our system. The 'debt bias' is increasing the returns on equity for the few who have it, but the negative impact on the use of equity finance overall may be having a much more damaging effect. Equity's ability to redistribute and recycle new wealth, to motivate employees and to bring valuable stability should be encouraged. Our tax systems do the opposite.

Crowded house

A part of my argument was always going to be tricky to deliver – and here it is. In the UK and the US especially, home ownership has become sacred; it is where debt has played the biggest direct role in most people's lives and, despite the crisis, most homeowners believe that financially speaking houses are – well – as safe as houses. There comes a point, though, when they're a cause of wealth inequality.

To be clear, home ownership has been a powerful force in the West, particularly in the US and the UK. It goes hand in hand with responsibility and so is an important stage of personal and social development; homes secure prosperity because they make people secure; they are a place to rest and rejuvenate. But too much focus on home ownership, despite its virtues, can crowd out ownership of other forms of wealth. In particular, it crowds out the ownership of equity.

As soon as most families owned their homes they were only a means to self-enrichment relative to the few who don't own a home; and, from that point on, rising house prices caused as many problems as they brought perceived benefits. The roof over our heads is a cost we bear to live and yet, when that cost goes up, we rejoice – the only cost for which we would. It is the illusion that debt is safe for both the borrower and the lender that has got us into this frame of mind. Generally, we look at the cost of a house as just the monthly cost of paying the mortgage, thus low interest rates make the house look cheap. If, however, the avail-ability of cheap loans is what's pushing up the price of the house in the first place, then, when all is added up at the end, we are no better off. The low cost of financing the mortgage is offset by the higher price we have to pay for the house itself. A circular process is in action: more credit to allow people to buy houses just leads to higher house prices and hence more demand for more credit.

Beyond a certain point, the rising price of houses leads them to soak up so much of the wealth that people might accrue through their lifetime that there is little room left for ownership of productive wealth. Nearly 70 per cent of the gross wealth of the US middle class is in the form of their principal residence; most of the rest is pension wealth, and yet, their average debt is actually more than both of those put together. For the top 1 per cent the opposite situation exists: only a fifth of their wealth is in their primary residence and pensions while they have around 80 per cent of their net wealth in business equity.[75]

Many commentators are on the case. Economist and journalist Anatole Kaletsky described the situation as a 'fraudulent inflation of property values and build-up of mortgage debt',[76] and yet politicians of all shades in the US and the UK have joined in the campaign to keep house prices rising – policies to keep them inflating and policies to help people into them are devised almost daily. So far it's working for them; at a conference in 2014 the Chair of the Federal Reserve, Janet Yellen, was relieved: 'Fortunately, rebounding housing prices in 2013 and 2014 have restored a good deal of the loss in housing wealth, with the largest gains toward the bottom,' she stated.

In the 1970s, Keith Joseph criticised the inflationary economic policies of his own party's Chancellor of the Exchequer, calling them a 'cruel deception on those whom it is trying to help'.[77] His sentiment may well apply to the housing boom today.

In the investment business, a particular term describes a situation in which all investors believe the same thing: a crowded trade. The crowded trade in housing may have a darker side than most of us appreciate. As well as crowding many people into houses that are over-priced, it's crowding most people out of ownership of equity. The investment business uses many great expressions, many of which ring true. It also, however, plays its own part in denying access to the real value of equity ownership.

Clipping coins

It's impossible to talk about denial in finance and yet ignore the financial industry. Except for houses, assets for the majority are acquired through the complex chain of advisers, managers, bankers and brokers who sit in the middle. Buying a stake in an 'apple tree', for most people, is an elaborate affair; getting the financial return is the same.

For example, let's say we want to buy some shares. We might go to a financial adviser for a recommendation and be told to buy a particular investment fund and pool our wealth with other people so that we can own a broad portfolio. The adviser will, of course, charge a small fee for the service. We then buy the fund and the fund manager chooses some companies that they think are worth investing in. They then ask a broker to buy the shares for them in the market, on an exchange perhaps. Over time the fund is paid dividends by the companies whose shares it bought, which, together with the increase or decrease in the value of those shares, is reflected in the fund's value. So far this sounds simple right? But so far I have simplified the process. In addition to the financial adviser, the fund manager, the broker and the exchange, there are custodians, nominees, investment consultants, funds-of-funds, retail platforms, distributers, high-frequency traders, dark pools, investment banks and many others sitting between our initial investment and the underlying asset.

They all take a small fee, which often looks miniscule at first, but they add up and compound. It's as subtle as the Romans' clipping of coins. If, at the age of forty-five, you invest £10,000 in a typical retail equity fund, a fund authorised to be sold to people other than merely professional investors, and leave it there until you retire, the asset management fees and underlying trading costs alone will be close to double the final return you receive yourself.[78] And this excludes the impact of high-frequency traders taking a clip, investment banks taking a return on their own books and a long list of other hidden costs that eat into the return

– in fact, most of the return. Tax incentives to invest through pooled schemes, pension funds and mutual funds have driven most investors into the hands of this complex web. In the US in 1945, nearly all shares were held by individuals; in the UK in 1970, 50 per cent of shares were held by households and, today, only 10 per cent.[79] One wonders, though, how many of the tax incentives actually accrue to the financial industry rather than the end-investors – a simple analysis tells us, the lion's share.

In his 1940 classic *Where are the Customers' Yachts?*, Fred Schwed Jr[80] pulled apart the self-serving complexity of the financial industry of the 1930s. Technology has moved on since then and we can now connect buyers and sellers of virtually anything, in any part of the world, almost instantly; and yet it seems the cost of taking our investment, putting it to good use and collecting the financial rewards has gone up not down. One US academic thinks these costs are higher now than they were at the turn of the last century.[81]

Few who buy assets through the mainstream financial industry understand the impact of complex and compounding fees; if they did, they wouldn't buy them. Is it possible, though, that one reason so few have actually invested is that they smell a bad deal?

Civic virtue

Our financial system is structured in such a way that it ensures just a few own the equity; our current approach virtually guarantees that ownership of productive assets, the most important form of wealth, is restricted to those at the very top of the financial pyramid. One might wonder whether this is important; so long as entrepreneurs with new ideas can invest and create jobs, that ownership is secondary.

For society, however, it does matter. The value that equity finance brings to companies, it brings to the economy as a whole. When widely used and broadly owned, it brings stability and a sense of shared endeavour that improves the outcome; debt finance, and the concentrated ownership it facilitates, does the opposite.

6
The Social Value of Equity

*Capitalism, then, is by nature a form or method of
economic change and not only never is but never can
be stationary.*
Joseph Schumpeter, 1942

At 7.10 a.m. one November day in 2002 I stood at
the front door of Morgan Stanley, the US investment bank where I had worked for three of the most
exciting years in stock market history. I called my wife
to explain what had happened. As an equity salesman
I had helped raise equity capital for a number of small,
mainly technology, companies; now the market had
died and I had been let go. I was a victim of the dotcom
crash.

Despite many casualties the dotcom bust failed to
derail the global economy in the way many thought
it would. More than half of the companies listed on
NASDAQ, America's main stock exchange for technology shares, didn't survive through 2004[82] and yet the US
economy was only in slight recession between March
and November in 2001. At the time, the dotcom boom
felt more like a bubble than the credit boom of 2007;
the mania was more tangible – you could almost smell

the tulips. One of the main reasons that explains why the global impact was nothing like as bad as that of the 2008 financial crisis, however, was that it was an equity boom not, at least mainly, a debt one. Although investors, professional and private, were all a little too eager, they sensed that the world was facing two of the biggest technological opportunities in a century, the World Wide Web and mobile communications. Given the massive and rapid movement in capital that these opportunities required, equity, in my mind, rose to the challenge.

With fifteen years of hindsight, many of the assumptions that equity investors made were in fact pessimistic. The glut of fibre-optic cable that spanned oceans, countries and cities was only a glut for so long; exponential growth in data traffic today makes many forecasts from the peak of the dotcom boom look laughably low. There was historic precedent. Consider railway speculation in nineteenth-century Britain, which left it with infrastructure that is still the backbone of its transport system; of 11,000 miles of track in use today, 6,000 was built in the boom period between 1844 and 1846.[83] When it comes to financing progress, history tells us it's better to be early than never. Some of the survivors of the dotcom bust went on to do great things. For example, when the bubble burst Amazon's share price plummeted from \$107 to \$7; at the time of writing, it's close to \$300 a share and Amazon has revolutionised the Western world's favourite pastime – shopping.

The UK's Astronomer Royal Lord Rees sees reasons to be optimistic: 'Twenty-first century technologies can offer everyone a lifestyle that requires little compromise on what Europeans aspire to today, while being environmentally benign, involving lower demands on energy or resources.'[84] New innovations will drive us forward but they will need finance to dream; as Keynes observed, 'individual initiative will only be adequate when reasonable calculation is supplemented and supported by animal spirits'.[85] Equity financiers, because equity shares success, can afford to dream, to summon up the animal spirits that Keynes talked of. Debt financiers, on the other hand, can only make *reasonable calculations*, and try to make sure they get their principal, the amount they loaned, back.

The bigger role of equity

We talk a lot about assets but we find it difficult to think about them outside of our own agenda. Pension funds think only of the risk and reward; corporations think only of the cost of their funding; regulators care about suitability for different consumers; advisers think about their revenue potential. Whenever we think about an asset, whether it's a bond, an equity share, a property or gold, more often than not we think first about the price.

Few people dwell on the role different assets play in society, how they motivate to create wealth, how they distribute wealth once created, how they influence the way we work together. Doing so requires some mental gymnastics; we need to study them from two different angles at the same time and we need to look from outside the system. In the case of debt and equity, they are both assets to own and, simultaneously, a source of finance for companies. They work, however, in very different ways.

In the first few months of 2014, American companies bought back more than half a trillion dollars' worth of their own shares, most of which will be cancelled. Modern financial theory justified their approach; they were using their balance sheets more efficiently. Although some investors were sceptical, the stock market generally celebrated – another buyer for your existing shares always looks like a good thing on the face of it. When viewed from the outside, however, one has a different take: the buybacks have taken half a trillion dollars of equity out of the system; they have focused ownership of yet more productive assets amongst fewer people; they have taken out of the American financial system another slice of its capacity to redistribute the returns to productive wealth, to spread the real returns of progress.

If users of assets don't think about the role they play in society, then it is the responsibility of governments to do so. It is their job, through regulators, central banks and taxation to incentivise the use of financial instruments that work better for society as a whole, not just the few. It is government's job to ensure that the financial system is not structured to benefit the few when that is not in the interests of everyone. I will return in the final chapter to what this might mean.

The Orchard 101

To accept the essential role that equity plays in society, one has to assume that equity for the economy as a whole, for all of society's productive assets, recycles wealth in the way in which it accrues the increasing value of a single asset. An assumption that some might dispute.

Let's go back to Debt and Equity 101 and look beyond the 'apple trees'. When assets grow, the increasing value is reflected in the equity. If we take this to the whole economy, one might say the 'orchard', then overall growth must be reflected in equity overall, right? Wrong – at least according to most economists. They'd say you can't treat the whole economy like a single company; they'd say there's an aggregation problem: it's not the same 'apple trees' each year. Some trees die and new ones grow, and so the owners of each tree may get more apples for a while but when the tree dies, they get wiped out – they only get extra apples because of the risk they take.

In aggregate, though, the rewards do get returned through the equity; in aggregate, they don't get wiped out; in aggregate, the owners always do better. Instead of owning one apple tree, imagine you own an ever-changing selection of trees, a portfolio, with some old fruitful trees and some promising new ones. Then the dying trees aren't a problem; the portfolio would evolve its way through the constant process of growth, maturity, withering and dying[86] that makes the orchard more productive for everyone.

Economic progress is an expansive tale of new growth, maturity, withering and dying; new ideas displace old ways of doing things, new products make old ones obsolete. Some people get caught on the wrong side of this process, they find themselves doing the wrong thing at the wrong time. The outcome, however, is a relentless rise in the value of the world's productive assets in total. The orchard constantly grows in size and value; there are very few occasions when it does not. A diversified portfolio of business equity is the only way to benefit financially, above and beyond the work we do. The more people in society who own such a portfolio, the more inclusive and stable our societies will be.

7
A Sense of Urgency

> *[I]f the shuttle could weave and the plectrum touch*
> *the lyre without a hand to guide them, chief workmen*
> *would not want servants, nor masters slaves.*
> Aristotle

If you want to vex an economist, tell him farmers don't grow apples, trees do. For most economists, labour is the prime mover of all creation – at least in the economic sphere. When we examine a farmer and their plough, conventional economic theory assumes that the farmer themself is made more productive as the plough becomes ever more sophisticated. Although modern ploughs are pulled by tractors that will soon steer themselves, guided by GPS through fields mapped by satellite, economic theory assumes that it is still the farmer being made more productive. From Adam Smith to modern neo-classical economists, it is an assumption that has rarely been questioned.[87] The main conclusion that follows this assumption is that, as labour productivity is endlessly enhanced, its wages in general will always go up; in aggregate, labour's share of national income should always remain the same.

For a long time it looked like this conventional

assumption was right; the more capital and technology we added, the more efficient labour became in general. The Luddites' distrust of machines and their fear for the lot of the English working class were laid to rest by their redeployment and the comforts that industrialisation eventually brought. Even when particular jobs were rendered obsolete, more often than not, new and better-paid ones turned up. With the exception of the occasional recession, labour's share of national income remained constant for most of the industrial era, a constant that became accepted as the norm up until the last few decades.[88] Equally accepted was the explanation that an 'invisible hand' was lifting up wages as technology made us all more effective.

Something is happening, though. Wages as a share of income have started to go backwards. The 'labour share' in the world's richest countries in 1990 was 66 per cent of national income; by the 2000s it was approaching 60 per cent.[89] While economic progress marches on, the rewards for work alone are stagnating. Increasingly those who own the capital – the factories, the research labs, the mobile phone networks, the social networks, all of the tools of prosperity – are taking more of the rewards. There are numerous explanations and, although so far the main one is cheaper labour in Asia and elsewhere, there seems to be something else at play too. As technology improves, the cost of investment goods – machines, robots, computers and the like – has started to collapse.[90] As well as getting faster, technology is getting cheaper. No longer is labour being enhanced by technology; it is starting to be outpaced and outpriced by it. Economists are unnerved; it looks like it might be the trees, not the farmers, that grow the apples after all.

The decline of the labour share of income holds two crucial lessons in relation to an argument against debt and the concentration of ownership I argue it enables. First, we should never accept even the most basic assumptions in economic theory as permanent, no matter who made them. All social structures, economies or otherwise, reflect the accumulated logic of scholars past but, every now and then, the logic breaks down; we should never take the theories that justify our reliance on debt, for example, as absolute. Second, if the balance between the returns to capital and the returns to labour is changing, then who owns the capital will matter more than ever. The proposals in this book will become an imperative.

The technologies behind robotics and computing are accelerating and colliding like never before; productive assets are starting to be productive without the involvement of labour. This is the case not in mature or declining industries alone, as in the past, but for the economy as a whole. If the only way to be rewarded in this new world is increasingly through ownership of productive wealth, then the problem of ownership, or the lack of it, may become much more real.

I have argued so far that extreme inequality in

wealth has been largely monetary, a result of extreme credit creation; from now on it might also be technological. Oxford researchers Carl Benedikt Frey and Michael Osborne think that 47 per cent of all jobs are at high risk of being replaced in the next twenty years.[91] Factory workers, lawyers, journalists, bankers, taxi drivers – the opportunities to cut humans out of work will be endless.

Erik Brynjolfsson and Andrew McAfee at the Massachusetts Institute of Technology have detected what looks like a new trend: following the end of the Second World War, US GDP and employment moved more or less in tandem; since the height of the dot-com boom, however, circa 2000, GDP has continued to rise but employment hasn't. It seems that in what they call *The Second Machine Age*,[92] the long-held fear that technology will make people redundant might now be coming true. They call it the Great Decoupling.

Technology will also bring an unusual twist to the story. While the financial system creates extreme inequality between the middle and those at the very top through concentrated ownership of equity, technology might hollow out the middle versus the bottom. It turns out that artificial intelligence finds hard things easy and easy things hard; a computer may give someone a loan or write a news article but it can't, even with the help of a robot, cook a meal, cut hair or maintain the garden. Modern technology might just hit middle-class professionals first.

Without an equity stake in the 'Second Machine Age' many more will become dependent on the state than we have ever imagined. The biggest risk is to dignity – those without ownership will be increasingly disconnected; welfare may offer sustenance but will never provide the economic freedom that comes from ownership.

Accelerating technologies will create a powerful and positive force for everyone. Who owns the 'apple trees', however, will matter more than ever.

Throughout the industrial era, few governments have concerned themselves with broadening ownership of productive assets. So long as industry had an adequate supply of finance to go about its business, for the formation of new wealth and the creation of jobs, then concentrated ownership was never seen as the most important issue. As wealth inequality now races up the agenda, however, how we finance our productive assets and who owns them will become an ever hotter topic. The traditional, and largely left-leaning, solution to inequality is ever more progressive income tax and confiscatory wealth tax[93] – it is the more obvious solution and one that most people can easily understand. There is a better way, however; one that maintains, or even enhances, the dynamism of capitalism while acknowledging that it has to be more inclusive; that a much greater proportion of society needs to have an economic stake in its future.

8
Beyond the Debt Bias

> *The dispersal of information about the economy and its opportunities across millions of people – with their different situations, different locations, different eyes and ears – is a given. ... We need also to facilitate, on top of that arrangement, a dispersal of control.*
> Robert Schiller, 2012[94]

To encourage the dispersal of ownership we need to re-think finance; we need to give equity a chance to breathe, to play a fuller role in our financial system. The incentives for corporations to use equity finance and for more people to own equity need to change – dramatically. Tax, accounting, the financial industry, central banks, financial education and culture all need attention or reform.

Any stockbroker will tell you that to arrange a deal between a buyer and a seller you need to have both sides of the trade. This simple principle should guide thinking on how governments accomplish an equity-based solution to our current dilemma. If we want more people to own equity, then we need to incentivise companies to use equity finance; conversely, if we want more companies to use equity finance, then we need to incentivise more people to invest in equity. Only in conjunction with its opposite will policy to tackle either side of the problem be effective.

Many doomsayers will say it's too late, that ever increasing use of debt is just too ingrained in the psychology of corporate finance and that investors' faith in the safety of bonds rather than the intrinsic qualities of equity is insurmountable. This often, however, talks to the doomsayers' intransigence rather than the intractability of the problem. There would, of course, be the need to question and abolish some sacred cows; sacred cows, however, are often a cover for vested interests. The crisis brought an opportunity to step back and look at our financial system afresh and, although to sceptics that opportunity seems to have been missed, that process has barely begun. Genuine structural change does, and should, take a long time; deliberation is the sign of a healthy democracy.

The road to an equity-centric financial system would take many routes and so this is no place for detail. Moreover, different countries face different challenges, with different systems and cultures; they will adapt in different ways. Without at least some broad prescription, however, this book would be a polemical rant and little else. If our premise is that the role of government is to ensure that the positive forces of capitalism work for everyone, then they need to incentivise the use of certain assets over others. This is not to say that they affect the relative price of assets, just that they should influence how finance functions.

There are three broad areas that would need to be simultaneously addressed: companies should be encouraged to use equity finance and routes to raising equity capital should be opened up; more people need to be encouraged and cajoled into owning equity; and, finally, we need to cut the cost of bringing the two sides together. Ultimately, there should also be a different approach from central banks and, although the magnitude and complexity of such a change is well outside the bounds of this book, one suggestion warrants attention.

Equity finance

The tax deductibility of interest for corporations is the elephant-in-the-room and the debate on its legitimacy has been going on for as long as it's been in place. The debate has been heating up, though. In 2005, a US presidential panel on tax reform proposed scrapping it[95] – somewhat predictably, the proposal was rejected. Since the financial crisis, economists at both the IMF[96] and the European Commission[97] have proposed reform to equalise the tax treatment of equity finance; so far, however, with the exception of one or two countries,[98] there have been few changes. In his wide-ranging review of the UK tax system, which proposed a shift in favour of equity finance, Cambridge professor and Nobel Laureate Sir James Mirrlees[99] is equally clear on the necessary changes but sees why they haven't happened: 'it is undeniable that some of the proposed changes would be politically difficult'.[100]

There are different ways to tackle the tax bias in favour of debt. In the extreme, we could cancel the tax deductibility of interest altogether, the so-called Comprehensive Business Income Tax, or we could allow for the cost of equity finance when determining a company's tax bill, an Allowance for Corporate Equity. Both have been researched in detail and both have pros and cons.[101] Either way, it's time to bite this bullet.

In the face of intense international competition for multinational companies to be headquartered in our own countries, removing the tax shield unilaterally might look like commercial suicide and, to be fair, an international treaty would be preferable. For any country, however, going it alone may not be as damaging as it might at first look. In 2007, US corporations, for example, paid $294 billion in corporate taxes but claimed $1.37 trillion in gross interest deductions.[102] Limiting the tax shield by 30 per cent would allow a reduction in the standard rate of corporate tax from 35 to 25 per cent while maintaining the overall tax take.[103] Corporations in general wouldn't be hindered, just those that use excessive debt.

Encouraging the use of equity finance without effective facilities in place for companies to access it would be fruitless; companies, particularly small and growing ones, need to be able to find equity capital more easily than they do today. Some countries are better than others; the US, for example, has a rich seam of business angels, venture capitalists and stock markets with a strong tradition of listing thousands of companies right down to very small ones. In the UK, on the other hand, less than 5 per cent of small companies report using external equity finance of any sort.[104] Tax plays a role here, as does the current financial industry,[105] but technology is our greatest hope of finding an enduring solution; equity crowdfunding, for example, is at a nascent stage but promising. These days most people are at home with the Internet; we like doing business on it – just ask Amazon. We also buy more and more of our financial services, such as insurance and banking, over the net so why not equity stakes in new and innovative businesses? The first small steps have already been taken with the arrival of platforms such as Crowdcube and Seedrs.[106]

In summary, governments should look favourably on the tax treatment of equity providers, consider carefully the structure of the industry providing equity finance and wholeheartedly encourage new technology and the firms that deploy it.

Broadening equity ownership

In 1973, Senator Russell Long, a Democrat, had dinner with Louis Kelso, a lawyer turned political economist who had been writing on the importance of broad capital ownership since the 1930s. It was a key moment for Kelso; for the first time since 1956, when he'd devised Employee Stock Ownership Plans, a scheme by which workers could acquire part ownership of the companies they worked for, a senior politician was taking him seriously. By 1974, Kelso's plan was enacted and today there are over twenty US laws promoting the use of ESOPs and over 10,000 companies[107] employing 13 million worker-owners[108] using them.

Apart from ESOPs, Louis Kelso's economic legacy has, so far, been marginalised. His belief, that 'if capital ownership is good for the rich, it is a thousand times better for the middle class and the poor',[109] however, provides a useful lesson for today's economic dilemmas. Once again, many countries are seeing the need for change. India, for example, introduced the Rajiv Gandhi Equity Savings Scheme. Designed to promote an 'equity culture', the scheme offers an attractive incentive, a 50 per cent tax break, for people on lower to middle incomes to invest in the stock market.

When it comes to investment, all countries' tax systems are a quagmire of different rates for different assets and different investors; comparing the investment tax regimes of individual countries secures the jobs of armies of tax accountants. If the West is to broaden ownership of equity, however, there needs to be radical change to the tax treatment of equity investors. The system should be designed, not to leave equity ownership as an afterthought, but to encourage people to own equity in established and start-up companies as early in their lives as possible. With respect to Europe in particular, the Chief Executive of the London Stock Exchange, Xavier Rolet, understands this well: 'Debt is tax deductible ... but risk capital is taxed at the corporate level, at the dividend level, at the capital gains level.'[110]

Pension funds play a crucial role in broadening ownership of equity. Along with life insurance companies, they are in a unique position when it comes to investment. Because their liabilities are normally in the distant future – they only return the funds they manage when their pension-holders retire – they can take a long-term view on the investments they make. And yet, for various reasons, they haven't used this strength.[111]

Pensions come in a myriad of shapes and sizes and, even for the most accomplished of experts, the advantages and disadvantages of different systems would take a lifetime to unravel. Actuaries, regulators, trustees, companies and unions look likely to remain forever locked in debate on the best solution. The steady shift away from defined benefit schemes, where the pensioner gets a fixed income on retirement based on their working salary, to defined contribution schemes,[112] where the pensioner's income depends on the investment performance of their fund, is in theory a move in the right direction. They give the pension-holder an upside to economic progress, to asset growth, rather than a fixed amount. In practice they haven't, so far, worked out that way. In general companies have not invested enough to deliver the income that pensioners would have received under the defined benefit system, investment performance has been relatively poor and the costs of administering the funds have been high. There is still much to do to ensure that such schemes are provided at a low enough cost and have enough exposure to equity.[113]

Despite being adopted in 1974, Louis Kelso's ESOPs haven't led to the revolution he imagined; more than 13 million Americans might participate in an ESOP but that's still a fraction of the 240 million people of working age. Similarly, in the UK only 6 per cent of employees own shares in the company they work for.[114] Not all initiatives on this front have worked. In 2012, for example, UK Chancellor George Osborne introduced tax incentives to encourage British companies to give shares to employees in return for dismissal and redundancy rights; only a handful of companies took them up. The conditions for such schemes to work are complex and their success often depends as much on a company's culture as it does on the financial aspects of the scheme itself. Governments can, however, influence their take-up; the dividends on shares held in onshore employee benefit trusts could be tax-free, for example, and capital gains on shares held by the trusts could also be free of tax. There would need to be strict conditions attached to such trusts; all employees should benefit, not just senior managers, and safeguards against their use for tax avoidance should be strongly upheld.[115]

Enhancing tax incentives to own shares is a tricky political exercise; very often they are seen as more a help for the rich than a catalyst for broader ownership. The popular image of equity ownership is still missing the core of what it truly represents: a stake in economic progress. In many ways this is down to the way the investment industry and regulators present it. The 2012 Kay Review of the equity market in the UK makes a good point on ownership: 'We regret that equity markets have evolved in a way which diminishes the sense of involvement which savers enjoy with the companies in which their funds are invested.' Rebuilding that sense of involvement is a crucial part of equity-based capitalism. Many government policies have tried to 'nudge' society's thinking on financial matters; the UK's introduction of a Child Trust Fund was, for example, a valiant attempt to develop a savings mentality. Convincing broader society that owning a stake in our shared economic future is not in any way elitist is vital to the solution to wealth inequality. Regulators around the world play a role in this respect and, in particular, they should approach the issue of risk very carefully; a thin line exists between protecting society from poor business practices and presenting risk as a one-way downward bet. Along with ensuring people who buy investment products understand the risks they entail, much effort should also be put into explaining the risk of no ownership at all; the risk of missing out on the returns that history, over a long period, shows are possible.

Returning the customers' yachts

For most people equity ownership will continue to be acquired through funds provided by the financial industry. The cost of doing so, however, will need to come down significantly if they are to be inspired to participate more than they do today.

A radical programme to ensure that investment is as low cost as possible should be put in place. Reconnecting broader society with productive assets means making sure that broader society gets the returns, not the finance industry. Once prudent ground rules for the industry are set, governments should encourage, even unleash, competition in every facet of the complex web of financial intermediaries that exists today.

Beyond quantitative easing

A discourse on central bank policy would run to several volumes but, given the ingenuity shown by central bankers' use of quantitative easing, there is one idea worth consideration that also supports the core thesis of this book.

Critics of current central bank policy argue that it favours the wealthy, those who already own the assets whose price is being inflated by quantitative easing. Many have argued that, rather than buying assets from banks to encourage lending, central banks should simply hand money out to everyone, especially the poor and middle classes who have a higher propensity to spend it and so to re-energise the economy. Ben Bernanke, who later became head of the Federal Reserve, even suggested this approach as a solution to the Japanese when their economy started to slow in 1998.[116] The policy, of course, is yet to be seriously considered by any central bank; in a 2012 speech, the Governor of the Bank of England Mervyn King argued that such a policy would be outside his remit as it was, in effect, a government transfer. In addition, the fear that such 'helicopter money'[117] would cause inflation, the deepest fear of any central banker, would prohibit such a crude initiative. There may, though, be a more sound approach to monetary policy which could work in the interests of everyone, rather than the few, while bringing sustained stability and growth to the economy.

There has been little inventiveness applied to the creation of credit mechanisms that support the ownership of equity; in fact, for the average citizen, banks will lend money for almost anything apart from it. This is ironic given that, as history tells us, it is, in aggregate and over a long enough time frame, the most creditworthy collateral any banker could lend against.

Rather than buying existing bonds (debt), central banks could establish zero-cost credit facilities that allow the general population to acquire equity. This could be done through the establishment of funds, or trusts, with the strict requirement that the underlying beneficiaries are locked in for at least fifteen years. Assuming a long-term return on the acquired equity of, say, 5 per cent, these trusts would be able to pay the central bank borrowing back within fifteen years and be left as owners of the acquired equity in full. The trusts themselves could invest in anything so long as it was through equity contracts, including private companies, infrastructure and new innovation. We would need to make sure the investment selection was not politicised and was left to professional investors driven by the need to deliver good returns; the allocation of units in these trusts, however, would be the decision of the government of the day. It could, for example, choose to distribute units equally, to means test their allocation, to give units to new-borns for release upon leaving school, or used to supplement the state pension with a funded scheme.

The strategy would have a number of positive effects. First, it would deliver a steady supply of fresh equity capital for corporations; with a higher supply of equity and lower supply of debt, they would then be more likely to use equity for the financing of new investment projects. Second, it would create a positive wealth effect in the economy, as citizens start to feel more secure about their retirement and have the value of their stake in these new trusts regularly reported to them; this would most likely stimulate new demand in the economy over time. Finally, it would create new wealth, new capital owners, without directly confiscating wealth from the existing ones; it would directly address extreme inequality in wealth and, in particular, inequality in equity ownership.

Conclusion

The word 'equity' comes from *aequitas*, the Latin concept of justice, equality, conformity and fairness. At large, equity is not just another form of finance; it is a way to get buy-in, participate, bring stability, build trust and optimism and create a greater sense of fairness. It aligns knowledge with control; it aligns interests. Equity in the financial sense incorporates *aequitas* in the ancient sense – it stands for virtues we cherish everywhere but in finance.

The move to an equity financed, rather than a debt financed, economy will require many vested interests to be overcome. Those who unfairly benefit from credit creation and tax bias in favour of debt, without doubt, will fight change. In the end, though, this is the simple choice we face: either we adopt the fairer, more inclusive and more stable system that more equity finance would bring or we stay on our current course until the social consequences of ever increasing wealth inequality force change upon us.

It would be easy to confuse the proposals of this book with pure laissez-faire capitalism but in practice they would need government right at the heart of the system, ensuring that finance is designed to broaden ownership not oversee its concentration. After the crisis, governments and central banks around the world had one main strategy: stimulate the flow of credit to the real economy, in particular to companies. Credit has indeed flowed; private debt is higher today than it was before the crisis. To tackle the problems we face today, however, it is not credit but equity that needs to flow.

America's fourth president and one of its Founding Fathers James Madison recognised the danger of narrow ownership: 'The proportion being without property, or the hope of acquiring it, cannot be expected to sympathize sufficiently with its rights, to be safe depositories of power over them.'[118] In 1829, he was talking about land; today, governments need to think the same way about equity.

Notes

1 Ancient Greek historian.

2 InequalityBriefing.org, Pay for middle-income earners is not increasing in line with economic growth (http://inequality briefing.org/graphics/57_IB_Ordinary_workers.pdf, 2012).

3 'The definitive guide to Britain's wealthiest people', *Sunday Times*, 11 May 2014.

4 Mount, F. *The New Few – or a Very British Oligarchy: Power and Inequality in Britain Now* (London: Simon & Schuster, 2012).

5 'Students Walk Out of Ec 10 in Solidarity with "Occupy"', *Harvard Crimson*, 2 November 2011. http://www.thecrimson.com/article/2011/11/2/mankiw-walkout-economics-10/.

6 Following the Third Lateran Council in 1179, usury – lending money at interest – led to excommunication. The Old Testament, however, offered a get-out for Jews: 'Unto a stranger thou mayest lend upon usury; but unto thy brother thou shalt not lend upon usury.' Jews might lend to Christians but not Jews. In 1516, the Venetian authorities designated a special area of the city for Jews on the site of an old iron foundry. In 1589, they were granted the status of Venetian subjects, although largely restricted to financial services. See Niall Ferguson, *The Ascent of Money* (London: Penguin, 2008), pp. 35–36.

7 Ridley, M. *The Rational Optimist: How Prosperity Evolves* (London: Fourth Estate, 2010), p. 12.

8 This is another simplification because if our income increases while we live in the house, then the imputed rental value to us, its utility value, might be said to go up also. In reality,

house prices have gone up way beyond their imputed rental value.

9 William, A. *The Successful Merchant: Sketches of the Life of Mr Samuel Budgett, Late of Kingswood Hill* (New York: Carlton & Phillips, 1853).

10 Dobbs, Richard, Lund, Susan, Woetzel, Jonathan, & Mutafchieva, Mina, 'Debt and (not much) deleveraging', McKinsey Global Institute, February 2015.

11 Confederation of British Industry, *Slice of The Pie: Tackling the Under-utilisation of Equity Finance* (London: CBI, 2014).

12 Handelsbanken, *Report and Accounts 2013* (London: Handelsbanken, 2013).

13 Admati, A. and Hellwig, M. *The Bankers' New Clothes: What's Wrong With Banking and What to Do About It* (Princeton, NJ: Princeton University Press, 2013).

14 Now the market knows it gets bailed out in a crisis, its debt is as safe as countries; their debt funding is way too cheap. Estimates on the size of the 'implicit subsidy' vary. The IMF in early 2014 estimated the global subsidy to be worth $590 billion (Global Financial Stability Report, IMF, April 2014).

15 Handelsbanken's return on equity has averaged 15 per cent; it was only slightly negative once during the Swedish banking crisis in 1992.

16 Turner, A. 'How to tame global finance', *Prospect Magazine*, 27 August 2009.

17 A quote from Shakuntala Devi, the 'human calculator' who was famed for calculating the cube root of 61,629,875 in her head.

18 People from the investment industry always like to talk about the best investments; it's like anglers and their fish. To be balanced, I also had my fair share of failures.

19 Capital Strategies, UK Employee Ownership Index (http://www.capitalstrategies.co.uk/index, n.d.).

20 National Centre for Employee Ownership (http://www.

nceo.org/articles/studies-employee-ownership-corporate-performance, n.d.).

21 Creaton, S. *Ryanair: The Full Story of the Controversial Low Cost Airline* (London: Aurum Press, 2004).

22 Blasi, Joseph; Freeman, Richard; Kruse, Douglas, *The Citizen's Share: Reducing Inequality in the 21st Century* (New Haven, CT: Yale University Press, 2014).

23 Ross, C., *The Leaderless Revolution: How Ordinary People Will Take Power and Change Politics in the 21st Century* (London: Simon & Schuster, 2011), p. 173.

24 John Lewis Partnership (www.johnlewispartnership.co.uk, n.d.).

25 Sandel, M.J. *What Money Can't Buy: The Moral Limits of Markets* (Boston, MA: Penguin, 2012). Sandel uses the extreme example of companies insuring against employees' deaths and taking the rewards when they die. The interests of both parties are not aligned by the market once moral questions come into play.

26 Of the 97 per cent of small companies in the UK that have not used external equity finance, most cite the loss of control as their biggest fear (CBI, 2014).

27 http://www.telegraph.co.uk/finance/newsbysector/media technologyandtelecoms/telecoms/11096384/Vodafone-blasts-Phones-4U-management-over-chains-collapse.html, 2014.

28 Proud, A. 'Why aren't the British middle-classes staging a revolution?', *Daily Telegraph*, 22 September 2014.

29 'Hail, the Swabian housewife', *The Economist*, 1 February 2014 (http://www.economist.com/news/europe/21595503-views-economics-euro-and-much-else-draw-cultural-archetype-hail-swabian).

30 Mattich, Alen, 'The German Exception to the Debt Explosion', *The Wall Street Journal*, 25 September 2014.

31 Technically speaking, GM filed for Chapter 11 of the US Bankruptcy Code.

32 The US government eventually recovered $39 billion when it sold its stake.

33 Warburton, M. *SAIC: GM Looks Well Positioned to Recover in China* (New York: Bernstein Research, 2014).

34 Data based on the 5th decile in terms of size, the middle, with growth in assets measured after issuance. See Didier, T. et al., *Capital Market Financing, Firm Growth, Firm Size Distribution* (Cambridge, MA: National Bureau of Economic Research, 2014).

35 Berman, K. and Knight, J. *Harvard Business Review* blog (http://blogs.hbr.org/2009/07/when-is-debt-good/, 2009).

36 Four scholars in particular shaped modern finance within just a few short years in the 1960s – all won Nobel Prizes. Modigliani and Miller's Theory of Capital Structure, William Sharpe's Capital Asset Pricing Model and Eugene Fama's Efficient Market Hypothesis are the cornerstones of Modern Financial Theory. Both M&M and the CAPM rely on the EMH as a starting assumption. Although all of these theories have been developed and complicated to cope with challenges to their basic assumptions, they still provide the basic framework for modern theoretic thinking about finance. When it comes to both corporate finance and investment management their basic conclusions are still the starting point for most practitioners. In its basic form M&M concludes that a company's value is unaffected by its financial structure; whether it uses debt or equity doesn't matter. CAPM assumes that an asset's return is determined by its risk that cannot be diversified away; risk is measured by volatility relative to all other assets, it's *beta*. The EMH assumes that markets are perfectly efficient and that all new information is immediately reflected in an asset's price. It relies on perfect information and 'rational' human beings to interpret it. The Efficient Market Hypothesis has defined modern finance and was taken as a given for decades;

statisticians poured over market data spanning years and concluded that the market looked like random noise, a sure sign that the Hypothesis was true, conclusive evidence that the markets were indeed efficient.

37 This is based on the so-called 'Prospect Theory' of Daniel Kahneman and Amos Tversky.

38 This excludes the debt of financials which, largely, is lending between themselves. Buttiglione, L., Lane, P., Reichlin, L., Reinhart, V., 'Deleveraging, What Deleveraging? The 16th Geneva Report on the World Economy', International Center for Monetary and Banking Studies (CEPR Press, 2014).

39 Graeber, David, *Debt: The First 5000 Years*. (New York: Melville House Publishing, 2014).

40 'On Being the Right Size', speech given by Andrew Haldane, at the Institute of Directors, London, 25 October 2012.

41 US household debt went from 16.9 per cent to 37 per cent of GDP. Before the Great Recession of 2009, US households' debt went from 49.1 per cent to 98 per cent. Kumhof, Michael; Ranciere, Romain; Winant, Pablo, 'Inequality, Leverage and Crises: The Case of Endogenous Default', IMF, 2013.

42 Buttiglione, Lane, Reichlin, Reinhart, V., 'Deleveraging'

43 'The Old Lady of Threadneedle Street' is a nickname for the Bank of England. It first appeared as a caption to a cartoon published in 1971 depicting William Pitt the Younger pretending to woo the Bank, personified as an elderly lady.

44 Fergusson, A. *When Money Dies*. (London: William Kimber & Co. Ltd, 1975).

45 The International Bank for Reconstruction and Development was later renamed the World Bank.

46 In practice, countries restricted capital flows to prevent speculation against their currency and so could at least keep some control over their domestic interest rates.

47 US Budget deficits had exceeded 2 per cent of GDP just three

times since the Second World War, by 1974 it was 3.2 per cent. Duncan, R., *The Corruption of Capitalism*. (Hong Kong: CLSA Books, 2009), p. 111.

48 Deng Xiaoping became leader in 1978.

49 The relationship between bond prices and interest rates is not immediately logical; the easiest way to think about it is to consider a so-called zero coupon bond which pays no interest but pays a fixed sum on maturity. For example, if a bond matures one year from now with a par value of £100 and the current price is £95 then the return from buying that bond, the interest rate, is 5.26 per cent ((100–95)/95 = 5.26). Now suppose the bond price rises to £98. At this point the interest rate is (100–98)/98 which is 2.04 per cent. As the bond price rose, the return, the interest rate, fell.

50 Divorces in England and Wales 2010, Office of National Statistics.

51 Keynes, J.M., *The General Theory of Employment, Interest and Money* (London: Macmillan, 1936).

52 The equity revenue also includes the rise of High Frequency Trading, which makes up a large part of equity income. Chappell, J., *Time to Change the Model* (London: Berenberg Bank, 2012).

53 Kay, J., *The Kay Review of UK Equity Markets and Long-term Decision Making* (London: Department for Business, Innovation and Skills, 2012).

54 Warren, A., 'The corporate interest deduction: A policy evaluation', *(Yale Law Journal*, 1974), 20, p. 1585.

55 Seager, A., 'Lamont paved the way to Brown's divi tax credit cut', *Guardian*, 5 July 2007.

56 Bloomberg, 'Corporate interest deduction proves sacred amid reformers: Taxes', 2013. http://www.bloomberg.com/news/2013-05-29/corporate-interest-deduction-proves-sacred-amid-reformers-taxes.html.

57 This was an argument put forward by Paul Krugman with

respect to US Government debt. Krugman, P., *New York Times* blog, 2011. http://krugman.blogs.nytimes.com/2011/12/28/debt-is-mostly-money-we-owe-to-ourselves/?_r=0.

58 And with the support of central banks, banks can do this ad infinitum.

59 Much of this debate relates to what economists call the aggregation problem. When they build sophisticated mathematical models of how we behave (what we buy, what price we'll pay, when we save, when we don't) and then add up all of our theoretical behaviour, it doesn't look quite like the economy we see reported on the ten o'clock news. Those that think the debt doesn't matter assume there is no aggregation problem, that the debt and the impact it has on debtors and creditors nets off to zero.

60 Various studies are discussed by Andrew Haldane in his speech 'On being the right size'.

61 Fergusson, *When Money Dies*.

62 This was the period of the so-called quantitative easing strategy, during which the Bank of England was buying bonds from banks and other financial institutions to free up their balance sheets so that they had greater capacity to lend to the real economy.

63 It took the economics profession six years to allow the two economists that discovered the Puzzle to publish their findings. Mehra, R., 'The equity premium: Why is it a puzzle?', Working Paper, February (Cambridge, MA: National Bureau of Economic Research, 2003).

64 ibid.

65 Barclays, Equity Gilts Study, 2014. https://wealth.barclays.com/en_gb/smartinvestor/better-investor/investing-lessons-from-114-years-of-data.html.

66 Private Pension Wealth, *Wealth in Great Britain 2010–12*, Office for National Statistics.

67 BNP Paribas.

68 Wealth in Great Britain 2010–2012, Office of National Statistics, 2014.

69 Wolff, E., *Recent Trends in Household Wealth in the United States: Rising Debt and the Middle Class Squeeze* (New York: Levy Economics Institute, 2010).

70 Rowlingson, K., 'Wealth inequality: Key facts', University of Birmingham, 2012. http://www.birmingham.ac.uk/Documents/research/SocialSciences/Key-Facts-Background-Paper-BPCIV.pdf.

71 Survey of Consumer Finances, Federal Reserve System, 2013.

72 Hall, J., 'Pension pots to plunge under new rules', *Daily Telegraph*, 12 November 2012.

73 Fernandez, P., *Ten Badly Explained Topics in Most Corporate Finance Books* (Barcelona: IESE Business School, 2013).

74 Mooij, R.A., *Tax Biases to Debt Finance: Assessing the Problem and Finding Solutions. Staff Discussion Note* (Washington, DC: IMF, 2011).

75 Wolff, *Recent Trends in Household Wealth*

76 Kaletsky, A., *Capitalism 4.0: The Birth of a New Economy* (London: Bloomsbury, 2010).

77 Joseph, S.K., 'Inflation is Caused by Governments', speech delivered Preston, 5 September 1974.

78 Research from Which? shows that if you invested £10,000 in a fund with no charges, and it grew by 6 per cent annually for 20 years, you'd get a return of £32,071 – just over £22,000 growth. If you invested in a fund with the industry average ongoing charge of 1.67 per cent, your return would be reduced to £23,344 – meaning £9,000 of your growth goes on charges. If the TER was 2.5 per cent, £12,000 would be paid out in charges.

79 Rydqvist, K., Spizman, J. & Strebulaev, I., 'Government policy and ownership of securities', *Journal of Financial Economics*, 2012, 111, p. 71.

80 Schwed, F. Jr., *Where Are the Customers Yachts? A Good Hard Look at Wall Street* (New York: Simon & Schuster, 1940).

81 Philippon, T., *Has the US Finance Industry Become Less Efficient?* (New York: Stern Business School, 2014).

82 Goldfarb, B., Kirsch, D., and Miller, D., 'Was there too little entry during the dot com era?' Robert H. Smith School of Business Research Paper, no. RHS-06-029, 2006.

83 Hancock, M. & Zahawi, N., *Masters of Nothing: Human Nature, Big Finance and the Fight for the Soul of Capitalism* (London: Biteback Publishing, 2011).

84 Rees, M., *From Here to Infinity* (London: Profile Books, 2011).

85 Keynes, *The General Theory of Employment, Interest and Money*.

86 In economics this is called creative-destruction, a term invented by Austrian economist Joseph Schumpeter.

87 Even Karl Marx used the assumption in the labour theory of value.

88 This is one of the six 'stylised' facts about economic growth defined by Nicholas Kaldor in 1957.

89 Organisation for Economic Co-operation and Development.

90 Investment goods costs have fallen by around 25 per cent in the last 35 years. Karabarbounis, L. & Neiman, B., 'The global decline of the labour share', *Quarterly Journal of Economics*, 2013, 129, pp. 61–103.

91 Frey, C.B. & Osborne, M.A., *The Future of Employment: How susceptible are jobs to Computerisation?* (Oxford: Oxford Martin School, Universtiy of Oxford, 2014).

92 Brynjolfsson, E. & McAfee, A., *The Second Machine Age: Work, Progress, and Prosperity in a Time of Brilliant Technologies* (New York: W.W. Norton, 2014).

93 These were, for example, the main policies recommended by Thomas Piketty in his bestseller *Capital in the Twenty-first Century*, (Cambridge, MA: Belknap Press of Harvard University Press, 2014).

94 Schiller, R. J., *Finance and the Good Society*, (Princeton, NJ: Princeton University Press, 2012).

95 *Simple, Fair and Pro-Growth: Proposals to Fix America's Tax System*. Report of the President's Advisory Panel on Federal Tax Reform, November 2005.

96 Mooij, *Tax Biases to Debt Finance*

97 Fatica, S., Hemmelgarn, T. & Nicodeme, G., *The Debt-equity Tax Bias: Consequences and Solutions* (Brussels: European Commission, 2012).

98 In 2008 the German government, for example, changed the rules so that, if a company's interest costs were too high relative to its earnings, if it had too much debt, then it could no longer deduct all the costs from its tax bill.

99 Mirrlees, J., *Tax by design: The Mirrlees Review* (Oxford: Oxford University Press, 2011).

100 Houlder, V., 'Mirrlees calls for sweeping UK tax reforms', *Financial Times*, 10 November 2010.

101 CBIT would increase the tax base and allow a cut in the corporate tax rate; ACE would narrow the tax base and need an increase in the corporate tax rate if it was to be tax neutral. There are other complications: the ACE would effectively give tax relief for super-normal profit ('rent') and CBIT may increase the overall cost of finance. In practice, the ideal is some combination between the two, depending on other dynamics in the country in which they are implemented; for example, ACE could assume a return on equity equivalent to the return on debt or a version of CBIT could limit the deductibility of interests only up to a certain point of leverage, a so-called thin capitalisation rule.

102 Pozen, R., 'Reform tax code by limiting corporate interest deduction', *Newsday*, 7 October 2012.

103 Ibid.

104 Confederation of British Industry, *Slice of The Pie*.

105 Even in the US where there is a developed market, fees for

raising equity capital in an IPO, for example, remain above 5 per cent of the total amount raised.

106 It is estimated that already in 2014 more than £80m of fresh equity capital was raised via crowdfunding in the UK alone ('Understanding Alternative Finance', Nesta, November 2014).

107 Centre for Economic and Social Justice, http://www.cesj.org/wp-content/uploads/2012/05/DinnerAtTheMadison1.pdf

108 National Centre for Employee Ownership, http://www.nceo.org.

109 Kelso, L.O. & Adler, M.J., *The Capitalist Manifesto*, (New York: Random House, 1958).

110 Hutchison, Clare, 'Europe should shake up tax rules to boost equity investment – LSE boss', Reuters, 29 October 2014.

111 Defined benefit pension schemes, for example, discount their liabilities at a rate equivalent to the yield on bonds. If, through QE, bond prices rise and yields fall, their liabilities from an accounting and actuarial perspective actually go up. The subsequent deficit often forces them to reduce equity holdings in favour of the perceived safety of bonds.

112 In the UK for example, only 14 per cent of Defined Benefit Schemes were open to new entrants in 2013, although 72 per cent of existing schemes were still on the old system

113 Recent legislation in the UK to introduce collective defined contribution schemes is aimed at providing more cost-effective pensions. Pooling workers assets and risk, in a way that is popular in the Netherlands, for example, will allow pension funds to invest in more equity and be more efficient in the administration of schemes.

114 Wealth in Great Britain 2010–2012, Office of National Statistics, 2014.

115 Offshore Employees Benefit Trusts have been the subject of much scrutiny in recent years. In particular in relation to misuse by companies making loans to employees against

payments made into them. This should not detract from the value of good tax treatment for genuine use.

116 Blyth, Mark & Lonergan, Eric, 'Print less but transfer more: why central banks should give money directly to the people', *Foreign Affairs*, September/October 2014.

117 The concept of 'Helicopter Money' refers to a thought experiment by economist Milton Friedman. In today's system it would comprise tax cuts paid for by printing money.

118 Blasi, et al., *The Citizen's Share*.

Bibliography

Admati, A. & Hellwig, M. (2013). *The Bankers' New Clothes: What's Wrong With Banking and What to Do About It.* Princeton, NJ: Princeton University Press.

Barclays (2014). Equity Gilts Study. https://wealth.barclays.com/en_gb/smartinvestor/better-investor/investing-lessons-from-114-years-of-data.html.

Berman, K. & Knight, J. (2009). *Harvard Business Review* blog. http://blogs.hbr.org/2009/07/when-is-debt-good/.

Blasi, J., Freeman, R. & Kruse, D. (2014). *The Citizen's Share: Reducing Inequality in the 21st Century.* New Haven, CT: Yale University Press.

Bloomberg (2013). 'Corporate interest deduction proves sacred amid reformers: Taxes.' http://www.bloomberg.com/news/2013-05-29/corporate-interest-deduction-proves-sacred-amid-reformers-taxes.html.

Brynjolfsson, E. & McAfee, A. (2014). *The Second Machine Age: Work, Progress, and Prosperity in a Time of Brilliant Technologies.* New York: W.W. Norton.

Buttiglione, L., Lane, P., Reichlin, L. & Reinhart, V. (2014). 'Deleveraging, What Deleveraging? The 16th Geneva Report on the World Economy'. International Center for Monetary and Banking Studies. London: CEPR Press.

Capital Strategies (n.d.). UK Employee Ownership Index. http://www.capitalstrategies.co.uk/index.

Chappell, J. (2012). *Time to Change the Model.* London: Berenberg Bank.

Confederation of British Industry. (2014). *Slice of The Pie: Tackling the Under-utilisation of Equity Finance.* London: CBI.

Creaton, S. (2004). *Ryanair: The Full Story of the Controversial Low Cost Airline*. London: Aurum Press.

Didier, T., Levine, R. & Schmukler, S. (2014). *Capital Market Financing, Firm Growth, Firm Size Distribution*. Cambridge, MA: National Bureau of Economic Research.

Dobbs, Richard, Lund, Susan, Woetzel, Jonathan, & Mutafchieva, Mina, 'Debt and (not much) deleveraging', McKinsey Global Institute, February 2015.

Duncan, R. (2009). *The Corruption of Capitalism*. Hong Kong: CLSA Books.

Economist, The. (2014). 'Hail, the Swabian housewife', 1 February. http://www.economist.com/news/europe/21595503-views-economics-euro-and-much-else-draw-cultural-archetype-hail-swabian.

Fatica, S., Hemmelgarn, T. & Nicodeme, G. (2012). *The Debt-equity Tax Bias: Consequences and Solutions*. Brussels: European Commission.

Featherby, J. (2009). *The White Swan Formula: Rebuilding Business and Finance for the Common Good*. London: London Institute for Contemporary Christianity.

Ferguson, N. (2008). *The Ascent of Money: A Financial History of the World*. London: Penguin.

Fergusson, A. (1975). *When Money Dies*. London: William Kimber & Co. Ltd.

Fernandez, P. (2013). *Ten Badly Explained Topics in Most Corporate Finance Books*. Barcelona: IESE Business School.

Frey, C.B. & Osborne, M.A. (2014). *The Future of Employment: How susceptible are jobs to Computerisation?* Oxford: Oxford Martin School, University of Oxford.

Goldfarb, B., Kirsch, D. & Miller, D. (2006). 'Was there too little entry during the dot com era?' Robert H. Smith School of Business Research Paper, no. RHS-06-029. https://www.aeaweb.org/annual_mtg_papers/2007/0107_1300_0904.pdf.

Graeber, D. (2011). *Debt: The First 5000 Years*. New York:
    Melville House Publishing.

Greenspan, A. (2007). *The Age of Turbulence: Adventures in a
    New World*. New York: Penguin.

Haldane, A. (2012). 'On being the right size', speech delivered
    for the Beesley Lectures, Institute of Economic Affairs,
    London, 25 October.

Hall, J. (2012). 'Pension pots to plunge under new rules', *Daily
    Telegraph*, 12 November.

Hancock, M. & Zahawi, N. (2011). *Masters of Nothing: Human
    Nature, Big Finance and the Fight for the Soul of Capitalism*.
    London: Biteback Publishing.

Handelsbanken (2014). *Report and Accounts 2013*. London:
    Handelsbanken.

Harvard Crimson. (2011). 'Students Walk Out of Ec 10 in
    Solidarity with "Occupy"', 2 November. http://www.
    thecrimson.com/article/2011/11/2/mankiw-walkout-
    economics-10/.

Houlder, V. (2010). 'Mirrlees calls for sweeping UK tax
    reforms', *Financial Times*, 10 November.

InequalityBriefing.org (2012). 'Pay for middle-income earners
    is not increasing in line with economic growth'. http://
    inequalitybriefing.org/graphics/57_IB_Ordinary_workers.pdf.

International Monetary Fund (2014). *Global Financial Stability
    Report: Moving from Liquidity to Growth Driven Markets*.
    Washington, DC: IMF.

John Lewis Partnership (n.d.). www.johnlewispartnership.co.uk.

Joseph, S.K. (1974). 'Inflation is Caused by Governments',
    speech delivered in Preston, 5 September.

Kaletsky, A. (2010). *Capitalism 4.0: The Birth of a New
    Economy*. London: Bloomsbury.

Karabarbounis, L. & Neiman, B. (2013). 'The global decline of
    the labour share', *Quarterly Journal of Economics*, 129.

Kay, J. (2012). *The Kay Review of UK Equity Markets and*

Long-term Decision Making. London: Department for Business, Innovation and Skills.

Kelso, L.O. & Adler, M.J. (1958). *The Capitalist Manifesto.* New York: Random House.

Keynes, J.M. (1936). *The General Theory of Employment, Interest and Money.* London: Macmillan.

Krugman, P. (2011). *New York Times* blog. http://krugman. blogs.nytimes.com/2011/12/28/debt-is-mostly-money-we-owe-to-ourselves/?_r=0.

Kumhof, M., Ranciere, R., & Winant, P. (2013). *Inequality, Leverage and Crises: The Case of Endogenous Default.* Washington, DC: IMF.

Mehra, R. (2003). 'The equity premium: Why is it a puzzle?' Working Paper, February. Cambridge, MA: National Bureau of Economic Research.

Mirrlees, J. (2011). *Tax by design: The Mirrlees Review.* Oxford: Oxford University Press.

Mooij, R.A. (2011). *Tax Biases to Debt Finance: Assessing the Problem and Finding Solutions. Staff Discussion Note.* Washington, DC: IMF.

Mount, F. (2012). *The New Few – or a Very British Oligarchy: Power and Inequality in Britain Now.* London: Simon & Schuster.

National Centre for Employee Ownership. (n.d.). http://www. nceo.org/articles/studies-employee-ownership-corporate-performance.

National Centre for Employee Ownership. (n.d.). http://www.nceo.org.

Office for National Statistics (2014). *Wealth in Great Britain 2010–2012.* London: ONS.

Peppers, D. & Rogers, M. (2012). *Extreme Trust: Honesty as a Competitive Advantage.* New York: Penguin.

Philippon, T. (2014). *Has the US Finance Industry Become Less Efficient?* New York: Stern Business School.

Piketty, T. (2014). *Capital in the Twenty-first Century*. Cambridge, MA: Belknap Press of Harvard University Press.

Pozen, R. (2012). 'Reform tax code by limiting corporate interest deduction', *Newsday*, 7 October.

Pringle, R. (2012). *The Money Trap: Escaping the Grip of Global Finance*. London: Palgrave Macmillan.

Proud, A. (2014). 'Why aren't the British middle-classes staging a revolution?' *Daily Telegraph*, 22 September.

Rees, M. (2011). *From Here to Infinity*. London: Profile Books.

Ridley, M. (2010). *The Rational Optimist: How Prosperity Evolves*. London: Fourth Estate.

Ross, C. (2011). *The Leaderless Revolution: How Ordinary People Will Take Power and Change Politics in the 21st Century*. London: Simon & Schuster.

Rowlingson, K. (2012). 'Wealth inequality: Key facts', University of Birmingham. http://www.birmingham.ac.uk/Documents/research/SocialSciences/Key-Facts-Background-Paper-BPCIV.pdf.

Rydqvist, K., Spizman, J. & Strebulaev, I. (2012). 'Government policy and ownership of securities', *Journal of Financial Economics*, 111.

Sandel, M.J. (2012). *What Money Can't Buy: The Moral Limits of Markets*. Boston, MA: Penguin.

Schiller, R.J. (2012). *Finance and the Good Society*. Princeton, NJ: Princeton University Press.

Schwed, F. Jr. (1940). *Where Are the Customers Yachts? A Good Hard Look at Wall Street*. New York: Simon & Schuster.

Seager, A. (2007). 'Lamont paved the way to Brown's divi tax credit cut', *Guardian*, 5 July.

Sunday Times (2014). 'The definitive guide to Britain's wealthiest people', *Sunday Times*, 11 May.

Turner, A. (2009). 'How to tame global finance', *Prospect Magazine*, 27 August.

Warbuton, M. (2014). *SAIC: GM Looks Well Positioned to Recover in China*. New York: Bernstein Research.

Warren, A. (1974). 'The corporate interest deduction: A policy evaluation', *Yale Law Journal*, 20.

William, A. (1853). *The Successful Merchant: Sketches of the Life of Mr Samuel Budgett, Late of Kingswood Hill*. New York: Carlton & Phillips.

Wolff, E. (2010). *Recent Trends in Household Wealth in the United States: Rising Debt and the Middle Class Squeeze*. New York: Levy Economics Institute.

Index